Enriched by
Him

Dot Goldie

Little Red Rocking Chair Publishing
littleredrockingchair.org

Enriched by Him

Copyright © 2014 by Dot Goldie

Cover and Book Design by: Maritza Cosano

All rights reserved. No part of this book may be reproduced in any form by any electronic or mechanical means including photocopying, recording, or information storage and retrieval without permission in writing from the author.

ISBN-13: 978-0-692-29096-5

Send your letters to the publisher,
Little Red Rocking Chair Publishing
LittleRedRockingChair.org
Email: Maritza@littleredrockingchair.org

Write to the author at:
dot@dotgoldie.com

Printed in U.S.A

Dedication

*This is dedicated to my Lord Jesus Christ.
TO GOD BE THE GLORY!
And to all the friends who helped make this book possible. To my editor, book designer and publisher, Maritza Cosano. To Sheila Powers for building my website. And to my long-time prayer partner, Maria Velarde, who witnessed some of the miracles recounted in this book.*

Introduction

I am so humbled that you've chosen to read my story, an odyssey that God began many years ago, but thankfully has not finished yet! If you read my first book, *The Encourager*, then you know that the last chapter ended with us waiting to hear from Calvary Chapel Fort Lauderdale on a decision that would send us, or not, to Hungary as missionaries.

Good news. We were.

And that journey was one that my husband Jim and I will never forget. I don't know about you, but every day that I walk with the Lord, I am reminded that He is an awesome God. *"For we are God's handiwork, created in Christ Jesus to do good works, which God prepared in advance for us to do,"* Ephesians 2:10.

In *Enriched by Him*, the story continues as Jesus guided us to the place of destiny. But unlike my first book, this one tells random life stories with no particular chronological order in mind. What you will see is a life purely based on faith. For even though Jim and I have planned along the way, it has been God who has directed our steps, showing us how to wait on Him so that we could see the big picture. Surely, He moved us onto maturity, teaching us to focus on the positive things, rather than exaggerate the negative, which could have led us to miss the good in every situation, and ultimately, His every blessing.

Has that ever happened to you? If it has, I can't emphasize enough too strongly how important it is that you resist the temptation to tap into your emotions and let it take control over you, or focusing on the negative, rather than the positive. That kind of thinking is no good. On the contrary, when you allow God to guide your thoughts through the studying of His Word— not only listening to what He has to say, but doing it—then you will see dramatic change in your life. If I may say so gently, it's time for Christians to truly step up. Figure out whom you want to follow. Jesus or the world.

Never one to mince words, the apostle Paul said it quite nicely in 1 Corinthians 1:10-17. In this passage, the Corinthians were acting like children as they were trying to decide whether to follow Paul, Apollos or Peter. "The question is whether or not you follow Christ! No one else matters!"

In other words, stop with the dramatics. Change your attitudes and way of thinking. Because when you set your minds

Dot Goldie

on filling it with good things, the result is always positive. Paul also gives us valuable instruction on this: "Set your minds on things above, not on earthly things."

Beloved, if you learn anything from my life, let it be this... thinking decisively to have total dependence on Jesus Christ is the principle of a good life, as He can only enrich it. Take a step of faith and watch a miracle unfold before your eyes.

Hungary

After much prayer and waiting on the approval process, Jim and I were officially missionaries on our way to Hungary. With our paper work done and mission cards printed, we set out to raise our support. Our friends were happy for us and encouraged us to continue our journey as we fixed our eyes on "higher things."

"You guys are perfect for this," they told us, and so that encouragement gave us the assurance that God wanted us to go forward with our plan.

The Bible states that because Abraham was "fully assured" about the promise God gave him, he did not waver or doubtingly question His instructions. Romans 4:20 - 21 says, *"Yet he did not waver through unbelief regarding the promise of God, but was strengthened in his faith and gave glory to God, being fully persuaded that God had power to do what he had promised."*

And so, we continued to meet with our missions pastor and others on the Calvary Chapel Fort Lauderdale missions team.

Dot Goldie

They told us to have a certain amount of money saved before we could go, as a way to ensure that we would not be caught short, but Jim and I felt like God was saying, *"GO! And I will supply all your needs!"*

Philippians 4:19 is my life verse. It says, *"And my God will meet all your needs according to the riches of his glory in Christ Jesus."*

You can see where I'm going with this… it was very hard for me to wait, even though that's what the missions team was telling us to do. In the meantime, we were receiving calls from Phil Metzger in Hungary. "When can you get here?" He'd asked.

"We have to wait until our leaders say we can go," we'd answer back.

Phil wanted Jim to go over there and be trained by a guy named Tom, who was leaving to California. However, the Calvary Chapel Fort Lauderdale's missions pastor still insisted that we wait until we had the set amount of cash before leaving.

So, we prayed, "Lord, where is the faith in this?" And, "Are you with us or not?" After much prayer about this, we asked for a meeting with the missions pastor. "We are willing to go with what we have," we told him, "We trust God for the rest. He will supply!"

God says in Hebrews 13:8, *"Jesus Christ is the same*

yesterday and today and forever." And we knew He would not go back on His word to us as our provider. Something I learned from this experience is that when you begin to conform to your way of thinking and living to God's Word, you will meet with a great deal of opposition, but you need to be firm to your decision, if you are certain that's God's will.

At last, the missions pastor relented and said, "Okay, you can go!" Immediately, we called Phil and told him we would be coming in June. We got our tickets and made arrangements to get all our passports updated, including our EU passports, as we have dual citizenship.

In the meantime, we were communicating with Dia at the college in Hungary. She was getting our paperwork done for our registration as residents in Hungary, and getting our medical records in place. The waiting had paid off, as the rest of the process went smoothly. All we had left was to pack up and say our goodbyes to all our friends and family.

It was a tearful time leaving our grandkids behind. But, as our daughter told us one day when she came over for a visit, "If I don't let you go, what is my witness going to be like?" She was having a hard time releasing us, but with tears streaming down her face she said, "I release you." Jim and I were filled with joy. I shared that morning's daily reading with my daughter.

It had talked about grandparents going on the mission field. Interesting, I thought. Normally it's the other way around; kids leaving for the mission field. So, it was confirmation for me that we were following Jesus' call to go.

God was very gracious to us. Our two sons also gave us their permission to go. They knew God had always worked in our lives over the years of serving Him and that this was just another "New Journey" God was calling us to.

"We give you our blessing," they said. What else can a parent ask for? That night, I thanked Jesus for our wonderful kids and grandkids. "How wonderful that they know and love you to allow us the freedom to serve you wholeheartedly," I prayed.

Living in a Castle
Where Else do King's Kids Live?

We arrived in Hungary on June 11, 2007, and served there for thee years. It was a blessed time for us. Jim was put in charge of maintaining this beautiful place where we lived.

The Castle, as it is called, is a huge Plantation type of building sitting upon 48 acres of land. The scenery around the grounds was breathtaking. The view behind the castle went on for miles overlooking rolling fields as far as the eye could see.

The colors of the fields were magnificent in the summer. Some were filled with huge sunflowers five feet tall or more. I know this because I stood beside some of them and they were taller than me! In the winter, it was like a fairyland covered in snow. The trees glistened in the sun as they were covered in ice. The roads were so beautiful to travel on, but oh, so terrible to drive through. God's beautiful creation surrounded us and it was an amazing place to be, knowing that it was exactly where God wanted us. I was put in charge of the coffee shop at first.

Dot Goldie

Phil thought since I am a people person I would fit right in. I had thought I was going to be the Teacher's Assistant for Calvary Christian Academy (CCA) for the little kids in 2nd grade. The school was still on vacation, so I agreed to work in the coffee shop.

Well, I can honestly tell you that I was not ready for all that it entailed. I had no knowledge of the monetary system. I had no training in making coffee like the way they make it at Starbucks! Plus, the language with some of the guests that were there for the conference, plus learning how to order stuff for the gift shop, etc.

I did my best with all of it up until the day I was left alone to do it all. That was when I had a slight heart attack, and it gave us all a scare. Phil recognized that the Coffee Shop was not for me.

"How would you like to be a TA?" He asked me.

I hugged him so tight tears flowed down my face.

"I don't want you dying on me on your first week!" He added, "You don't have to work in the Coffee Shop anymore."

I was a happy camper after that. By the way, I had a procedure done in the hospital in Budapest. I never had a problem again with my heart from that day to this day, Praise the Lord!

Holy Spirit Came Down… In my Kitchen!

God did many wonderful things with the kids at CCA Hungary. I taught 2nd through 5th grade Bible class for over the three years, and during that time I saw them grow so beautifully in the Lord.

Things were going along as usual until one night. As I was preparing my lessons for the next day, God spoke to my heart.

"This is what I want you to teach," He said, and then proceeded to lay out a program for me to follow. I wrote it all down on paper until I had the picture of what He wanted. This came as no surprise to me, as I had been struggling with the curriculum that I had been given, mainly because the kids were disinterested, and quite honestly, so was I!

I spoke to Phil, as well as Paul Lang, who was the head of the school at the time. I showed them what I had and they gave me permission to go with it. I bought each of the children a "Daily Journal" and asked them to write out their testimonies.

That was the first thing!

Dot Goldie

Every day we would start our lesson with a time of waiting on the Lord, followed by prayer. Interesting thing, during the time of waiting, the kids began to "hear God."

I had instructed the kids to keep their journals open on the table, so that if they saw or heard something from the Lord, they would write it down or draw a picture. The kids loved this part of our class, and so did I! My favorite time was actually when we got to share what the Lord had given each and every one of us.

If I ever started a lesson without our time of "Waiting," the kids would say, "Miss Dot, we have to wait on the Lord first!"

One morning, I was teaching them about the baptism of the Holy Spirit. During our waiting time the Holy Spirit fell upon us, one by one. I was blown away.

I sat there, tears running down my face. Judah, the Senior Pastor's son, who was only eight years old, began to speak in tongues! After each time he spoke there was a second of silence, then he proceeded to interpret what he said. This happened three times.

After Judah finished speaking, two other boys, Ian and Sean, had words of knowledge. Sean, 10 years old, said that the Church in Budapest was going to have a night of waiting for the Spirit to come upon them and that the whole church would be blessed. Ian, 9 years old, who was the quiet one of the two, received a word for one of the students up at the college. Ian knew who she was and so, during lunchtime he went and gave it to her. She fell apart crying. She had asked the Lord for direction, and Ian had delivered His answer.

That morning, while this was taking place, my husband Jim came walking into the kitchen, and immediately was aware that God was doing something. He walked out quickly, careful not to disrupt what God was doing. Afterwards, when the kids left to go to their next class, I called Sean's mom to tell her what had happened. When she heard it was me on the phone she said, "Oh, no! What has Sean done now?"

"I have some amazing things to tell you," I told Jeanette. "Sean was baptized in the Holy Spirit this morning. He had a vision for the church and was interpreting as well as speaking in tongues!"

"Paul and I were praying at ten o'clock for Sean," she said in total awe, as that was when the Holy Spirit came upon us. Sean called Phil to tell him what he had said for the church in Budapest, but he was not answering his phone. At lunchtime, Phil came back to the castle, so I went over to his table and told him what had happened that morning. I tried to write down as much as I could remember of what Judah had said, then showed it to him.

"This is not the words of an eight year old," he said after he read my note. We praised the Lord together!

"Continue teaching your curriculum and encourage the kids to keep listening to the Lord," he said. I nodded, in total agreement with his orders.

Later, Phil got that morning's message on his phone. He was speechless. "No one knew that I had planned to have an evening of 'waiting on the Lord' for an outpouring of His Spirit," he said, and so we were all in awe of what God was doing.

I continued to teach the kids, watching with delight how the younger ones drew pictures in their journals. Some were not proficient yet at writing, so this was the best way for them to express themselves creatively.

One morning, Kara, five years old, was drawing in her journal while waiting on the Lord. She was scribbling like crazy with a black crayon covering the whole page, but for a tiny corner where she drew a yellow-filled circle. When I went around the table asking the kids to explain what they had drawn, Kara said, "The darkness was trying to put the Light out, but it won't go out because Jesus is the Light!"

You could have blown me over with a feather. Charis, five years old, who could write but not spell too well, wrote a song and then sang it to me. Leah, eight years old, wrote a song too and sang it to me, but hers had actions to it! Jim was blown away too. "I could feel the presence of the Lord this morning," he said, as he walked in on us.

Jim was not the only one who witnessed this incredible movement. All the pastors were witnesses to all that I have written. We were all amazed at what God did in our midst.

I could go on and tell you of all the things that God did during that time I had with these kids, but it would take another book to write it all down. For instance, Judah had a vision of the house that the Metzgers were going to move into in Budapest.

Color and everything!

His parents were blown away.

Another part of my curriculum was to get the kids to write to a missionary who was in prison in Mexico for having a gun in his rented house. The gun wasn't his and he never knew it had been there. Still, the police targeted the pastor because he was a Christian and was leading people to the Lord.

I received an e-mail about this, and though I didn't know who this pastor was, I decided to get the kids to pray for him. We contacted his wife by e-mail and told her we were going to pray for her and her husband, as well as for their family. She was thrilled that some kids on the other side of the world would be praying for his release.

Dot Goldie

"I was only allowed to visit him and take a mattress for him to sleep on," she said. "I'll keep in touch with you to let you know how my husband is doing."

Every week, the kids and I sent her a prayer to take to her husband. Soon, this turned into a huge relationship. We found out when he was going to trial, and so we kept praying.

One day, Judah said, "The pastor is getting out of jail," and then wrote to the pastor and told him the day of his release was coming. The pastor had not even had his trial date set yet, but it happened just as God had told Judah.

When the day came for the pastor's release, he asked to stay another few days because he was preaching to some men that were in prison with him. He wanted to make sure that they were saved before he left. The pastor was released a few days later and he wrote a letter to my kids, thanking them for praying for him and his family. He also wrote a newsletter and mentioned my kids. "Some elementary children in Hungary prayed for my release and God honored their prayers," he wrote.

*****

Years before I went to Hungary, I used to work with a teacher named Cherie at Coral Springs Christian Academy in Coral Springs, Florida. We stayed connected throughout the years and one day I received an e-mail from her husband Steve, telling

Enriched by Him

us that Cherie had cancer. We prayed for her as a class, and the kids also wrote to her. I knew Cherie would appreciate this as she always encouraged her students to write to others in need as well.

The kids wrote her prayers and also told her how they were doing in school. She wrote back and forth to them until she couldn't do it anymore. But, Steve asked if we would still write and pray for her, as he would read the letters to her.

We did this for several months. Then it happened again! Judah heard God say, "Cherie is going to be alright!"

It was just before Thanksgiving when we placed a call to her.

"You are going to be home for Thanksgiving!" Judah told her.

"Judah, I want to be home by Thanksgiving, but I am not sure if the doctors will let me go home," she told him.

Well guess what?

Cherie went home the day before Thanksgiving!

I don't know about you, but God has shown me to believe:

"To him who is able to do immeasurably more than all we ask or imagine, according to his power that is at work within us," Ephesians 3:20.

Being His Messenger

Have you ever asked Jesus, "What do you want me to do for you?" If you have, you have probably heard His answer. As for me, God has communicated a simple mandate: be my messenger. Sometimes He has given me specific messages to pass on to people, even those I didn't know that well, like in the case of Phil and Joy, a missionary couple living in the castle.

One night, during service at the castle, the Lord told me to pray for Phil. They hadn't told anyone that they were moving to Budapest to be closer to the church, where Phil was the senior pastor at the time. Every day I would lift him up in prayer before the Throne of Grace and one day the Lord woke me up and said to me, *"Write this down for Phil."*

It was about three in the morning!

I got up and wrote down what I heard and then began to pray for the right time to share this word with him. I didn't know how Phil would take it at first, but I went over to their house later on in the day to give it to him.

Enriched by Him

Phil was not home, so a sigh of relief washed over me.

I'll just give it to Joy and leave, I thought.

"I want you to please read it to Phil," she begged and continued by offering me a cup of tea. "He's over at the Foster's house and will be home any minute," she said. Just then Phil came bursting in through the door.

He looked at me and said, "Hi Dot! What's up?"

"She has a word from the Lord for you," Joy said. "She wants to read it for you."

But before I could do anything, he grabbed it out of my hand. "I'll read it myself," he said and sat down on his chair and began to read what I had written.

"Oh, yes! Thank you, Lord!" He said over and over until he finished reading. He looked up and fixed his eyes on me and said, "This is what the Lord has been talking to me about!"

Then to my total surprise he said, "Dot, if God gives you anymore things for me I want to hear them!"

I was so relieved to hear that. The Lord had used me to deliver His message at other times and with other people, but I hardly knew Phil at this juncture in my life. As the Lord talked to me about Phil, I prayed for him and he very graciously accepted my prayers. Then, one day the Lord showed me that Phil and Joy were moving. I wrote this message down, but I did not want to deliver it, because I didn't want them to leave! On this particular day Joy asked me, "Has the Lord given you anything for us?"

I hesitated.

"Has the Lord told you we are leaving?" Joy whispered in my ear.

"Yes," I said. "Several weeks ago."

"Can I read it?" She asked and I nodded. I went to my house and brought the note to her.

"No one knows anything that we are moving," she cried after she read the note. "This is conformation that we are on track with the Lord's plan for our future."

News traveled fast and everyone was amazed, especially me. I was so blessed to be able to pray for them and to give them the encouragement they needed. Funny thing was, I was being encouraged as well. Phil made a journal of all that the Lord spoke to him through me, and as far as I know, it has all come to pass. *Praise God!*

Years later, as I was writing this book, God spoke to me about Phil. So, I wrote to him in Hungary, sharing what the Lord was telling me from the book of Daniel.

I wrote: "God is going to bless you through this word." Phil e-mailed me back saying, "Wow! How timely, as usual! Thanks, Dot." God is so good.

Discovering My Voice

Speaking in public is not something that I would have chosen to do if given the option. Can't think of anyone who would naturally choose that, but then again we are all wired differently. I wasn't. Not then, that's for sure!

Despite my fears, I discovered my voice by simply letting God use me to help and encourage as many people as I could. The first time I spoke in public was for a group of women in Scotland. I shared what God was doing in my life as a houseparent to 17 kids in a children's home that my husband and I had in Broadstairs, Kent, England.

One time I was at a church in England and they asked me to share about Mr. Fegan's Children's Home. I have to be quite honest, I was a bit long winded and some of the old people were nodding off as I was speaking. As a matter of fact, I remember an old gentleman who sat in the second row even snored! That could have stopped me from speaking again, but I laughed it off and put it down to inexperience.

Dot Goldie

After we had been in America for a few years, I returned to Scotland for a short visit with my parents. While there, I visited our missionary friends Bill and Margaret Gilvear. Bill had asked me to go with him to a Woman's Guild meeting, where he was going to preach.

"Dot, can you lead worship or share a little of what God is doing in your life?" He said, and I was terrified. But then, Bill prayed for me and I was good to go.

Bill was my mentor in the faith. He showed me by example how to walk the walk, as well as talk the talk. "Give God the glory in everything," he said, and that was the best advice he ever gave me. I loved his teachings and learned so much through them, especially how to be bold and speak up for Christ.

A friend of mine told her church leadership about me and asked them if I could come and share at their women's retreat in Daytona Beach at El Paraiso Hotel. They agreed and welcomed me into their fellowship with open arms, and it became an annual event for four years in a row.

One day, my senior pastor ran into one of the leaders of that church and asked him, "How did things go at the women's retreat?"

"The church has been set on fire for the Lord!" the leader

Enriched by Him

exclaimed, and I had to laugh when I heard that, as my friend Dawn always calls me "The Fire Starter" for some reason.

I believe The Lord wants us to live in holy expectancy so we can receive His best. This attitude can ignite a fire within so strong that you are always able to give and help change other lives. Perhaps that's the fire that my friend Dawn sees. Still, I don't consider myself a fire starter, but a small wooden stick God uses to bring light into a situation. Very much like a match. Friction from striking a match produces a flammable compound, which then ignites in the air. The two chemicals needed to produce the reaction are present on the match head and the striker. Similarly, God uses us [the match] to create friction and ignite a fire that produces a vibrant flame—the Body of Christ.

During one of those speaking events, I invited some ladies from my church to come with me. I wanted them to share their testimonies and get used to sharing in public.

I have learned that any day that we get to share Jesus' goodness with others is a good day. But first, we need to let go of our fears and allow God to use our stories to help others.

A funny thing happens when you share your testimony. Most women would say that they are willing to love and pray for anyone, but are not too quick to speak out loud in public. Making the decision to share intimate things you have never communicated to anyone is not always easy. But I can tell you that it can be liberating. This was the case for the women who went along with me on this trip. The Holy Spirit radiated through them, giving them the courage to be bold and minister to other women as they shared their stories of redemption and faith.

The conferences were powerful because of these women's boldness. The way I see it, life is too short to waste one day without sharing our faith. I believe God showed up mightily in these conferences to remind us that He gives His love freely to those who want it, and there's no better time to seek the Lord than today.

As I prepared for each conference, I would ask God to show me if there was anything He wanted me to share with these ladies. He began to give me a picture of different people, and a specific word for each one. I wrote it all down and when I came up to share, there they were… in the audience! I saw their faces and called them out, providing the word that the Lord had given me for each of them. They were all amazed, and so was I!

This was the beginning of what God began to do through me as I opened myself up to Him to do whatever He wanted to do through me.

"I was praying in my quiet time and I saw you wearing a blue plaid outfit," I shared with one of the ladies later that night.

"I had laid out two outfits to bring with me and had them on my bed wondering which one to wear tonight," she said as she broke down crying.

"Wear the white one," her roommate had said.

"I'm convinced now that the Lord was speaking to me," she said, "the word you gave me was right on!" The next evening she wore her blue plaid outfit!

The Lord blessed many of these ladies. Some got saved and some were filled with the Holy Spirit. There was this one lady who was delivered from fear and unbelief after I talked about this very thing. When I quoted 2 Tim 1:7, which says: *"For God has not given us a spirit of fear but of power of love, and a sound mind,"* this woman went running out of the room screaming.

Everyone looked on, wondering what was wrong with her. The woman's friend went after her to comfort her.

Yes, I could see the sparks were flying.

"Let's pray for her," I said, as the Lord led me to calm the rest of the women and continue on with my message.

Later that night, I sought her out and found her feeling terribly guilty for making such a commotion.

"I am so ashamed," she said.

"We prayed for you," I said calmly. "Can I pray for you now?"

She agreed, and so I prayed following God's direction,

Dot Goldie

"Lord deliver her from her fear and unbelief in her life." After the prayer she sighed and surrendered her life to Christ. Praise God!

I had many more meetings like that in other women's conferences. My team members and I went forward to do the job that God had called us to do.

"Speak up. Spread my Word. Ignite the fire until my return," He pressed, and we're still doing that.

Something I realized in my travels is that women, in general, are the same wherever you go. Sure, their cultures may vary, but deep inside, regardless of whether you are an America, African, European... we struggle with similar fears and opposition. I remember this place called Kapisvar in Hungary. I was asked to speak and my friend Kriszta was my translator. She was very good and often translated for the pastors at the Bible College.

Kriszta had a good grasp of my Scottish accent, and so she was well prepared for some of my Scottish sayings and translated it very well.

I shared with these ladies what God had done in my life and how He was and always would be my Jehovah Jirah—my Provider.

I noticed some of the ladies had tears running down their faces as I spoke. Later I asked Kriszta, "Why are they crying?"

Enriched by Him

"They didn't know that God could do things like that in their lives!"

"My faith in God has become greater now," Kriszta recalled some of the ladies saying. "I can trust God for things in my life, believing that He will do for me what He did for Dot."

This was my purpose, I thought. This is what the Lord had created me for—to encourage others, to spark the flame that's inside of us, and see lives changed from glory to glory by the grace of our wonderful, amazing, all powerful, Almighty God.

Pre-Kindergarteners...

Gotta Love Them!

Jeanette was a pastor's wife. She was from Sweden and the mother of three great kids, her youngest being Jake, or as I liked to call him, Jake Bear. Now Jake was a handful.

One fine day Jeanette came to my door and as I opened it she said, "Here, take him!" She plopped the squirming three-year old into my arms and then walked away.

Poor Jeanette had had it with him. He wouldn't behave, so she told him, "I'm taking you to Grandma Dot. She will sort you out!"

I didn't think I had that kind of reputation, but I guess I did. Jake calmed down with me. I had him for about three hours that day until Jeanette got herself together again. She knew how I dealt with all the kids at the castle. I did not tolerate tantrums. Not from kids, not from parents.

"I'm so sorry, Dot," Jeanette apologized to me when she came to pick up Jake that day. Her husband Paul was teaching

Enriched by Him

and Jake had been acting up all morning.

"I just lost it," she said, "I don't know what I would have done to him."

"I didn't mind," I told her. I'd held onto him until he'd stopped crying. When he calmed down we played for a while with the few toys I had for the kids to play with. When he got fed up with the toys, he started to jump on the couch and I gave him my look.

He stopped.

He knew he was not allowed to do that in my house. I never had a minute's trouble with him that day. When the kids came to my house I didn't let them run wild or jump on my furniture. I simply said, "No!" and they stopped.

Soon they learned that if they came to my house they had to behave and do what they were told. If they did, they got to have a fun time with Grandma Dot!

I baked cookies with them and let them get their hands into the dough and roll it out. Then, we would very carefully put them in the oven to bake. When the cookies were ready, we would have afternoon tea.

The kids loved that!

They knew too that I kept a jar of "sweeties" in my cupboard. (That's candy for you Americans!)

The kids would knock on my door and ask, "Can we please have some gummy bears?"

If they did not ask properly and be polite and say, "Thank you," I wouldn't give them the candy.

One day, Jake and Hannah, the other three year old, knocked on my door to ask for candy.

Jake said, "We want sweeties!" and as quick as a flash, Hannah nudged him and said, "Please, may we have some sweeties, please?"

I said to Hannah, "You may have some, but Jake didn't ask properly. You know how I like nice manners."

Jake jumped up quickly and said, "Please, can I please have some sweeties, please and thank you?" all in one breath.

I bit my lip, hardly controlling myself from laughing aloud. The moment was PRICELESS!

I gave them both their Gummy Bears. Working with pre-kindergarteners had its precious moments. Often I would ask them, "How old are you?" or I would say, "Hold out your hands," making them count with me as I placed three Gummy Bears into each of their hands.

"Thank you Grandma Dot, until the next time!" They said.

They were so funny.

Enriched by Him

I really loved those kids; they were so precious to me. They loved me too, even though I wouldn't let them have their own way. Their parents appreciated it too. I was teaching them early on to have nice manners so that whenever they went out anywhere they would be polite.

God's Amazing Knowledge

One day Jim and I were praying for people after church service and this couple came up to us asking for prayer. They did not tell us what was on their mind except that they wanted God to help them. As Jim was praying for them, the Lord gave me a picture to share with them.

"Hold out your hands with your palms up to allow the Lord to take away your problem," I said as I looked at them both directly into their eyes. "The Lord says, 'Let everything go! Release it all into My hands.'"

That was it! They thanked us and walked away.

Three years later, we came back to Calvary. I was walking down the aisle when I bumped into this man.

"Do you remember me?" A man named Frank asked.

"I do!" I answered. "How are you doing?"

Frank then told me his story. He and his wife were in the IT industry and had invented something, but one of the big computer companies had stole it from them. They had been trying hard to get it back, but they had been intimidated by the company's big lawyers. The night Jim and I prayed with them, they had released everything into the Lord's hands.

Frank wanted to tell us this but didn't know we were missionaries in Hungary. He had looked for us but had never been able to find us, until now.

"We wanted to tell you that God had worked it all out and we got a lot of money from that company when we settled out of court!" Frank later told us.

"That night when you told us God wanted us to release everything, that was the answer we were looking for," explained Frank.

"We were holding tightly to what we thought was ours but God showed us that it wasn't ours, but His, and that He would work it all out for His Glory, if we would let go and allow Him to do His part in all that was going on!"

What a story! You just never know how God is going to use the words of your mouth when you open it wide enough to let Him fill it.

"*I am the Lord your God. I rescued you from Egypt. Just ask, and I will give you whatever you need,*" Psalm 81:10.

I did this many years ago when I first read this verse. I opened my mouth wide and said, "Lord you fill it." As I prayed, the Lord showed me the picture of a huge big spoon and his hand holding it, and letters were coming off the spoon into my mouth. I will never forget that. I can still see that vision in my mind's eye. The Lord never fails to amaze me.

As he says in Habakkuk 1:5, *"Look and be utterly amazed For I am going to do something in your days that you would not believe even if you were told."*

My answer to the Lord is, *I believe you, Lord!*

Frank and his wife Cindy are now good friends of ours, and we often get together for dinner at either of our houses.

What a God we serve, there is none like Him! Amen? Amen.

Lord, I pray for anyone right now that is reading this and going through some difficult times that You would be to them what You have been for us. You don't play favoritism, Lord. So, please do for them what You have done for us. In the name of Jesus. Amen.

It's true. God doesn't play favorites. But He does expect we put Him first. This idea appears in the Bible numerous times, but one that comes immediately to mind is Matthew 6:33: *"But seek first his kingdom and his righteousness, and all these things will be given to you as well."* In other words, if we put God first, all our needs and desires will be met; everything else in our life will fall into place.

Just Do it!

Just do it! The Lord instructs me every day. Nike has had that slogan for years and millions of people follow it. But as for me, I follow the Lord's call to step in faith, and every time without fail I have seen His faithfulness when I do. In 2 Timothy 2:13, we are reminded that, *"If we are faithless, he remains faithful, for he cannot disown himself."*

The thing is, the Lord is not looking for sacrifices, just plain obedience. I found this out when He asked me to write my first book. I told Him I couldn't do it, that I didn't have the time, that I was not a writer. *What was He thinking? I asked.* And yet, here I am writing my second book.

I am not doing this to make money or anything like that, although it would be a blessing if anyone was led to donate to our vision for Missionary Care. The profits of the books will go to missionaries in need all over the world.

Being a missionary is not easy. Missionaries sometimes get lonely out there in the mission field overseas. A little tender loving care helps keep them on the field, and it helps all of us step out in faith, believing God is in the business of miracles, especially for those people whom we support and pray for.

I encourage you to make a time in your daily walk to wait on the Lord for instructions for your day. Whatever He says, just do it! Don't rush out into your day and leave Him behind and then as a second thought when things are not going too well, call out to Him for help.

Put God first in everything you do. And give Him the first of everyting, because when you do, you are saying, "Lord, before I do anything else, I want to give you the first portion of it back—not because You need it, but because I want to thank you for giving it to me first. I trust You to take care of me and meet all my needs." So, give God the best part of every day by spending time with Him before you do anything else. Give Him the first portion of your finances and watch Him bless the rest. God is good. He is our God! He deserves our best. Think: "I will put God first in my life." Then, just do it!

Now, before you go out into the world, put on the whole armor of God. Pray the blood of Jesus over you for a covering from the attacks of the enemy. Be obedient. And if you are, you will feel the presence of the Lord with you when you just do it! His promise is to never leave us or forsake us.

The Dentist with a Soft Touch

Have you ever found a dentist with a soft touch? I have. I met Dr. Al Brecher when I first came to the States. Our whole family needed treatment but we could not afford it. And so, that's when Dr. Lunsford, an orthodontist friend of ours, referred us to him. I dreaded what I was going to be facing, as I had always been deathly afraid of dentists, but asked the Lord to please go before me. I arrived at the office and was greeted by the receptionist with a big smile.

"Hi! How are you?" She said.

"I am here to see Dr. Brecher," I said, trying to muster up courage.

"Please, sit down, I will tell the doctor you are here," she said and moments later the dentist came out to the waiting room.

"Hello, so I see you come highly recommended by Dr. Lunsford," he said.

I thought to myself, *I come highly recommended to you? Should it not be the other way around?*

Dot Goldie

Dr. Brecher, a small Jewish man, took my hand in his and said, "I will not only take care you, but your whole family!" He proceeded to tell me in detail about all the treatments that he would be providing for everyone in my family.

"I'm sorry, I think there's been a mistake," I said, thinking I had missed a step. "We cannot afford all that treatment."

He held out his opened hands and said, "If I can't help you then I can't be called a Christian."

Here was this gentle, little Jewish man telling me, someone he didn't really know, that he was going to provide free dental treatment to a family of five. Unbelievable. But, that's our God. He does things like this for His children all the time, and I was not about to start arguing with the Lord. Not on this, anyways!

My first treatment was over before I knew it. Dr. Al Brecher was so gentle. "If Jesus was a dentist, then I reckon this is how His handy work would feel," I told him afterwards and he smiled humbly. My family felt the same way as they received his gentle, dental care. Later, as we got to know him, he became known to us as "The Doc." Jim did some remodeling in Doc's house, and so that made us feel like we were able to do something in return for all the good he had done for us. Our friendship with the Doc grew and it was a blessing to have him in our lives.

At that time, we were going to New Covenant Church, but

Enriched by Him

the Lord had been moving in our hearts that we had to leave there and find another church. It was during one of our visits to the Doc's office that he told us about his church.

"Our pastor has been baptized in the Holy Spirit and things are going great," he said. "I think you should come and visit."

"Al, I think we will," Jim said, and so we went the following Sunday to see if this was the place for our family to come and worship. It was. We joined the church the next Sunday and went to Al's weekly Bible study, where we met several new people. When they found out I played guitar they invited me to lead worship for the group each week.

Those were fun times. And, I never had any fear of going to the dentist ever again! Al, as we now called him, took care of us for many years and did not charge us for any of the treatments he provided for us.

Sometime later, Al went on a mission trip to Africa and contracted some germ from the water. He got very sick and the illness took a toll on him. During that time, there was an outbreak of Aids in Africa. It was all over the news that a dentist had contracted the disease and had infected some of his patients. This did not go well for Al. With him being sick and in the hospital some of his patients dropped off, even though he didn't have Aids. People just got scared and left. After that happened, he wrote us a letter saying that because he had lost so many patients he would have to charge us half price for treatments from now on.

"Even if you charged us full price we will not be going anywhere else," we told him. In fact, when Jim got insurance to go to another dentist we stayed with Al, even though he did not take our insurance.

Clearly, Dr. Al Brecher is going to have lots of gems in his crown to lay down at the feet of Jesus when he sees Him in heaven. I thank the Lord every day for bringing this gentle man and his precious wife Bobbie into our lives. Bobbie and I did a couple of retreats together where God used her Jewish background to bless many who were Jewish and help lead them to their Messiah Yeshua.

It never fails to amaze me how God brings people into our lives from all walks of life, and it's like we have known them forever. It's going to be great when we all meet together in heaven, where we will never be separated from each other again. We'll worship our Lord together, rejoicing in His presence forever and ever... and without translators. Imagine that!

No One Can Steal My Joy

Back in London, during the time when we were at the children's home, every now and then we would get interviewed by social workers who wanted to place children in our home.

Martin Granger was the social worker for Fegan's House and he brought two ladies to our home to visit, and to see if our home was a good "fit" for the children they were hoping to send to us. I made my usual afternoon tea with scones, jam and whipped cream for our little get together. The conversation went well until it turned to what Fegan's was all about.

"We share the Gospel of Jesus Christ and winning souls for Him," I explained to the two women, and then continued by sharing my testimony. I could see that they were shocked by what I was saying and by the way we ran the home. I pressed on. The Holy Spirit was leading me and there was no stopping me.

They asked me questions about my faith and I answered. Jim jumped into the conversation, backing me up and showing that we were a team as we loved and disciplined the children.

Dot Goldie

"You have too high a standard for these kids," one of the women said, with her proper English accent.

"It's not my standard but the Lord's," I quickly replied. "He has called us to look after these children and to teach them that they should obey the Truth, who is Jesus Christ. We attend church services every week and they are involved in Christian activities for their age group during the week."

I shared the gospel after that. At one point in the conversation I turned to Martin and asked him, "Are you not going to stand up and be counted?"

I challenged him to speak a word but he never did.

"Dot, I know you are full of froth and bubble, but I can take that away from you!" Martin said after the meeting.

"No man can steal my joy in the Lord and I pity anyone who tries!" I said and then ran upstairs to my bedroom. I sat down at my dresser and cried my heart out, then prayed with my head down on the dresser with my hands on my head.

"Lord, please forgive me for the way in which I spoke to Martin before he left the house," I prayed, and just as I did, I heard the Lord's voice speak to my heart.

"They did it unto me before they did it to you!"

It was so real I was afraid to look up in case I saw the Lord standing there beside me. I felt the pressure of His hands on my shoulders as I heard these words. I did not want to move an inch! I wanted to stay there as long as I could just sitting in His presence. The peace that came over me was indescribable.

"Call Martin and ask his forgiveness," I heard the Lord tell me in my heart. So, I lifted up my head and looked in the mirror. I honestly thought I would see the Lord standing there, but I didn't. I got up, washed my face, and went downstairs to the office to call Martin. Jim was on the phone. He was speaking to Martin, who was at the other home just a couple of miles away from us. He was telling Jim something he had forgotten to tell us. I motioned to Jim that I wanted to speak to him when he had finished their business.

"Martin, I am so sorry for the things I said," I pleaded with him. "Please forgive me?"

"I forgive you," he said. "I need your forgiveness too. I didn't know how to speak my faith out the way you did when talking with the two social workers. So, will you forgive me?" I did and our relationship was restored. We prayed for one another.

Jim had no idea what was going on, so I told him and then he also rejoiced. God is so good. He did a work in all of us that day, including the two social workers, who sent a family of three to come live with us at Little Dumpton. Praise God! No one can take away my joy! John 16:22.

The Day I Went to Heaven

I attended a leadership conference with my pastor and other church leaders. One morning, after being refreshed in the Lord, drinking in all the teaching and seminars, we began a prayer meeting. A few of the elders stood up and prayed, while soft piano music played in the background.

The presence of the Lord was in the room. I closed my eyes and listened to the prayers. Suddenly, their voices began to decrease while the music began to increase in my ears. The Lord's presence and peace was all around me when all of a sudden I felt like I was floating away.

Was this heaven? I wondered. I could see myself standing before a hazy, bright light, which was surrounded by rays of color. Out of this incredible brightness the form of a man appeared. Somehow, I knew it was Jesus. He came and stood beside me, but I could not see His face because the light was so bright. He never spoke to me, but led me around this place, motioning with His hands as He pointed out to places as if to say, "This is yours." He knew my thoughts and answered my questions, one by one even before I had a chance to speak them out.

"This is where you are coming," I sensed Him saying. "This is all yours," He repeated, pointing to everything around us. The whole place was gleaming; the walls sparkled by what I could only imagine were precious gems. I saw what looked like a wide river of glass. The street I was on seemed like gold, so smooth and shiny. We walked down this road and then it came to an end. I looked back and was about to ask, "Where are all the people?"

Suddenly, I could hear music, loud music but not hurting to the ears. I could hear singing. Loud, happy, joyful singing! All of a sudden it was as if a balcony came down from somewhere and all the people were leaning over it and calling out to me saying, "This is where you are coming! You are coming here!"

The voices disappeared and I was back in front of what it appeared to be a throne immersed in bright light. As I was trying to adjust my eyes, I felt Jesus' hand on my back. *"Now you have to go back and tell them I am coming soon,"* He said. *"Tell them this is real. It does exist. Go back and tell them."* He gave me a gentle push, but I resisted.

"I don't want to go back. I don't want to leave!" I said and again I felt the gentle push on the small of my back.

"*Go back and tell them that heaven is real,*" Jesus said.

I did not want to go back. I cried and cried until the next thing I knew I felt a bump!

I was back in my seat.

I opened my eyes and felt the wetness on my cheeks. I turned to my pastor and saw a deep question in his eyes.

"Where did you go to?" He whispered.

"I was not in my seat," I whispered back. After the prayer meeting ended, I told him what I had experienced. My feet hardly touched the ground as I walked with him and his son on the way to lunch.

Like John the apostle, I don't know if I was in the Spirit or in the flesh, but I do know this: I saw Heaven and all the glory in it, and the Lord Jesus gave me a personal tour of it. I will never forget that day, but mere words could never describe what I saw and heard that day. It was all too glorious, too perfect and true. I praised God for His goodness and grace for letting me a get a glimpse of heaven.

Later that week, I shared my experience with Jim Goll, who was one of the pastors at the conference. He led me to Revelation 4:1-6, which says: *"After this I looked, and there before me was a door standing open in heaven. And the voice I had*

Enriched by Him

first heard speaking to me like a trumpet said, 'Come up here, and I will show you what must take place after this.' At once I was in the Spirit, and there before me was a throne in heaven with someone sitting on it. And the one who sat there had the appearance of jasper and ruby. A rainbow that shone like an emerald encircled the throne. Surrounding the throne were twenty-four other thrones, and seated on them were twenty-four elders. They were dressed in white and had crowns of gold on their heads. From the throne came flashes of lightning, rumblings and peals of thunder. In front of the throne, seven lamps were blazing. These are the seven spirits of God. Also in front of the throne there was what looked like a sea of glass, clear as crystal. In the center, around the throne, were four living creatures, and they were covered with eyes, in front and in back."

I was speechless, perhaps for the first time in my life. Then Jim read Hebrew 12:1, *"Therefore, since we are surrounded by such a great cloud of witnesses, let us throw off everything that hinders and the sin that so easily entangles. And let us run with perseverance the race marked out for us."*

I recounted these verses in my mind, never before having seen them in this way. Jim interpreted what I had just experienced and to this day, whenever I read this passage of Scripture, that glorious day plays like a video in my mind.

Dot Goldie

It took me a while to tell anyone else other than these few leaders at the conference. I thought people would think I had just made it up. But then, I remembered what Jesus had told me, *"Tell others that Heaven is real."* And so, I did.

I don't know why God would bless me in such a way, but I am eternally grateful that He did. All I can say is, I can't wait to go back!

Mondays with Maria

My friend Maria is a quiet Spirit-filled Peruvian. Mother of two and grandma of three, we have lots in common, and we have known each other for over thirty years. Our Pastor had suggested to the congregation that we should "team up" with a prayer partner to pray for each other and the body of believers.

My husband Jim and I were part of the prayer ministry at our church, and as usual after the church services, we would walk up to the front of the church to pray for those in need of prayer. It was during one of those times that we met Maria.

"Can you please pray with me for my young son," she asked. I don't know why, but as she came near I quietly asked her, "Would you be my prayer partner?" Her face lit up.

"I wanted to ask you to be my prayer partner but thought you probably had someone else already," she said. So after church that night we talked and made plans to meet on Monday mornings at 9 A.M. for about an hour.

How wrong we were! Our times lasted from 9 A.M. to 3 P.M.,

stopping only for a lite lunch, then it was back to prayer. We sang some of the time; I played the guitar, and the Lord would just bring things to our minds to pray about.

Maria and I shared deep personal things with each other that no one but Jesus knew about. Mondays with Maria became a huge blessing in my life. We met faithfully every week come rain or shine, and together, we watched God move powerfully in our lives as we enjoyed His presence. On occasions, one or the other would have a visitor from Scotland or Peru, but that did not stop us from meeting for prayer.

It is a powerful thing to have another person in your life to share absolutely anything with them, knowing that it will go directly to the Throne Room in intercession on your behalf.

That is my friend Maria.

It really amazed everyone around us that Maria and I had such a relationship. It could only have come about because of God. We were, as the saying goes, "Different as chalk and cheese."

Folks would laugh and ask, "How do you two understand each other?" Maria has a very strong Spanish accent; I have a very strong Scottish brogue. We knew that God had put us together and we had *no problema* understanding each other! That's my best Spanish.

Enriched by Him

Mondays with Maria lasted for more than 10 years, until the Lord moved me on to another place. During that time, we saw God do miracles in our families and in the lives of those He sent to us for prayer. Many people came to us in church and asked if they could join our prayer time.

"Yes, of course you can. Come!" But they would come for an hour and then leave. Our pastor asked us if we would move our prayer meeting to the church and get some others involved. We did this and soon it grew into a full-blown prayer time. Men and women would join us; it was an amazing!

After ten years, from the night when our pastor asked everyone to find a prayer partner, Maria and I were the only original pair left. To this day, Maria and I are still prayer partners and best friends.

Maria and I met up again after Jim and I returned from Hungary, and we now have a missionary prayer meeting every Tuesday night at our house and both our husbands have joined us.

September 11, 2001

The horrific news flashed on our TV screens. An airplane had crashed into the World Trade Center in New York City. Everyone was struck with shock. An invading enemy had hit us hard. Then a few minutes later another plane crashed into the second tower. The world looked on in disbelief. Then the Pentagon, symbol of American might, was hit by hijacked American flight #77 from Dulles at 9:38 A.M. in Washington. And yet another plane was struck in Pennsylvania.

What's going on? I wondered, and I wasn't the only one asking that. As the world looked on, the images of the World Trade Center, following the terrorist attacks on the United States, September 11, 2001, left one of the most indelible memories in the collective psyche of Americans, and the world. That unforgettable day has stayed with us ever since.

A couple of weeks after the attacks, Owen, our youth pastor, who was from New York, felt the Lord calling him to go help. He asked the congregation if anyone would like to be part of

Enriched by Him

a ministry team and fly up to New York and help with the clean up, or whatever needed to be done. Jim and I felt led to go, so we signed up right away after the service. We were not the only ones. A large group gathered and we were to join forces with the Salvation Army.

Our assignment was simple. Help at the site, feeding the firemen and the police officers, who were going through the debris, looking for bodies still buried under the rubble.

Before setting off, we were invited to a meeting to get our job details. Jim and I were thrilled at being chosen to be part of this first mission team to go from our church. We had never been to New York. And although it had always been a dream of ours to go, we had never imagined our first time would be under these terribly sad circumstances. Our assignment was to serve at the morgue from 7 P.M. to 7 A.M.

"The rest of the team might not want that," explained our youth pastor. "And since you are older, I believe you may be able to handle that schedule better."

I was a bit disappointed when I heard our assignment. I thought, *We will be up all night and sleeping all day!* We wouldn't be able to see anyone or anything.

How wrong I was. The Lord is always so gracious. He never withholds any good thing from those who love and serve Him.

Dot Goldie

Finally, the day came when we set off on Jet Blue Airlines to New York. The group was ready, and although we hardly knew anyone on the team, we soon became very close. The men did all the heavy lifting of bags and beds, as we were going to be sleeping on the floors at Grace Fellowship Church in Manhattan. The church building was undergoing remodeling, so the place was a bit of a mess. It had a huge cross, which lit up and read, *Jesus Saves*. Across the street was the Post Office and down at the end of the street was Madison Square Garden, the world's most famous indoor arena in the heart of Midtown Manhattan.

The guys slept on one side of the balcony in the church, and the girls were on the other side. There was another room where about six of us slept on the floor in our sleeping bags. Some people had airbeds, while others had cots, and the rest roughed it on the floor. It was a mish mash of people everywhere! There were two bathrooms and one shower for about eighteen girls. The men had no problem, but maybe it was because some of them didn't even bother to shower!

Our mission was clear and the realization of it hit us hard. And so, in the midst of everything, we could not even think about the basic necessities such as bathing. Our team meetings took place in the small Sanctuary and our fellowship times were in another room that had tables and chairs, and rats the size of

Enriched by Him

cats! One day, I just happened to look over at what I thought was a cat and was shocked to see that it was the biggest rat I had ever seen. I know everything is big in the USA, but this rat took "the biscuit," as we say in Scotland.

On our first day, we were to get our passes to enter "the site," or wherever we were going to be working. The Salvation Army people were organizing all this for us. Everything was going well, until it came to my turn to get my badge.

The machine broke down.

"You will have to come tomorrow," they said.

"But I can't do that! I'm working at the morgue tonight," I replied, feeling a bout of nervousness.

"You will not be allowed to go into the morgue unless you have that badge," said Owen, upset at the situation. We sat down and prayed.

"You're going to have to come tomorrow," said one of the Salvation Army officers.

We kept praying. "God, please, make it work for one more badge!"

"One more, Lord! One more badge, please!" I prayed.

We all went into the room where the man was working on the machine. He looked up and then continued doing his thing.

"We are praying for one more badge to come out of the

machine," we told him. We laid hands on the machine and prayed over it. "Can you please try it one more time?" We asked him and he tried it once more. Then, Lo and behold! The badge with my photo on it popped right out. The other teams that were waiting for their badges were delighted to see this happen because they too could not come back the next day. I got my badge, hung it around my neck and everyone rejoiced with me. Then man working at the machine went back to get the next team's badges but the machine broke down again. Unfortunately, the others did not get their badges that night.

Later that evening, we went to the morgue. We walked all the way in the pouring rain and freezing cold, but I was happy to have my badge. I was ready to go to work. There were four of us on that nightshift team. Jim and I, and two other guys.

When we finally reached the morgue, we had to go through several security checkpoints before we were allowed to go to our assigned jobs. Jim and I were assigned the "Lunch Truck." The two other guys were assigned the "Tent," where they were to serve snacks and sodas. There were tables and chairs with TVs for the firemen and other workers who could come in and relax when they had time off to do so and have a light meal or a nice snack. Meanwhile, Jim and I had this huge grill and several great big giant coffee pots to serve grilled cheese sandwiches or other deli type of food. We worked all through the night to serve police officers, firemen, cleanup workers and medical examiners who came to our truck for coffee and sandwiches.

I took the opportunity to witness to every single person that came to our window. I shared the Gospel with each one and prayed for them before they left with their coffee and sandwich. On a couple of nights, a Salvation Army officer came to help us find our way around the place. It didn't take long before he offered us a position with the Salvation Army! Of course, we declined. He said, "We need people like you in the Army that share the Gospel like you do."

Several people accepted the Lord as their Savior the week we were there. One police officer rededicated his life to the Lord as we prayed and ministered to him. I will never forget that night.

It was pitch black outside, pouring rain and freezing cold. The man came for a 'white coffee, no sugar' and a grilled cheese sandwich. He was shaken up by all that had happened and the reports that continued to come in, listing 3,497 people dead, including 343 firefighters, 37 Port Authority police officers and 23 New York Police Department officers. This officer had lost several of his friends at the World Trade Center.

One of the Salvation Army officers had given us a special

Bible for policemen and firemen. "Give it to whoever you think might use it and read it often," he'd said. So Jim and I asked the Lord if this was the one we were to give this Bible to.

"I have fallen away from the Lord and have lost all interest in church," the officer said and as we listened to him, the Lord laid it on our hearts to give him the Bible. We prayed with the officer and he rededicated his life right there in the pouring rain.

Joy came over him, and his whole countenance changed.

"I feel a weight has just lifted off of me!" He said, as a smile brightened his eyes.

Praise God!

That same night a janitor accepted Jesus as his personal Savior. Then a medical examiner came by and she got saved too. What a night that was! We were elated to say the least. Time flew by and soon it was time to go "home" to the church.

We walked home on a "HIGH" in the Lord that morning! When we reached the church, I bid Jim good night, even though it was morning. We parted to go to our side of the balcony to our sleeping quarters. The day shift was up and getting ready to go see the sites before their shift started. As for me, I was tired. I went downstairs to the bathroom, where all the ladies were primping their hair and getting their makeup on. I just wanted to get a shower and go to sleep. I had been up for 27 hours by

Enriched by Him

that time. I had brought my wet jacket with me to throw into the drier that was down there. I popped it in as all the ladies were leaving. They all said "goodbye" and left me on my own. I was about to jump into the shower, when all of a sudden the lights went out. The drier had caused a fuse to burn out.

I was in the pitch dark! I could hear the scraping of the rats scurrying around, so I grabbed a little flashlight that I had in my jeans pocket and pointed in front of me. Sure enough, there they were.

Rats!

I threw my robe on and ran out of there as fast as I could. I caught sight of Jim.

"Lights out and so are the rats!" I said and then explained to him what had happened. He reported the outage to the church people and the lights were fixed.

Needless to say, I never took another shower by myself again unless another person was down there with me. I just washed my face at the sink and got out of there.

That morning was not over, though.

I went up to the room where I had left my air bed and sleeping bag to find someone else sleeping in it. Talk about Goldilocks! The girl was sound asleep. She was not going to work until 10 A.M. Oh, how nice.

"What should I do?" I asked another woman from our team, who took me to another room.

"You can use the mattress that's on the floor and use the sleeping bag that's on it," she said. I was too tired to do anything else, so I slipped into the bag and was getting "comfy" while a couple of girls were getting dressed to go sightseeing.

"Do you girls mind putting the light out and maybe go into the next room?" I asked politely. They did and were very nice about it all.

I was just falling over to sleep when another girl came into the room. She put the light on and began shouting for her friends.

"Can you please put the light out and be quiet?" I asked softly. "I need to get some shut eye." She apologized and left.

Finally I was on my own. I talked to the Lord for a wee while, thanking Him for all He had done the night before, then I dozed off, only to be awakened by a women singing a hymn in the Sanctuary. It was the church's morning prayer time.

People were shouting Hallelujahs and Amen for about an hour! Then, they left. I no sooner was getting to sleep again when I awoke to the melodious sound of a jack-hammer ripping up the church floor in the basement. Remember, they were remodeling the whole place. What a night! What a morning!

Enriched by Him

It was as if the enemy himself was trying to discourage me after such a glorious night of people giving their lives to Christ. I prayed, and believe it or not I actually fell asleep.

Before going to work that night, we asked Owen if he could speak to the pastor about the prayer meeting. He did, and they moved the meeting to another location. The jack-hammer was finished now and it was only the sound of a hammer banging nails.

The next night, as we walked down to the morgue, we bumped into another team member who was returning from his shift at the "Hole," as we called it. This is where the Twin Towers used to be.

"You two are the ones that gave a Bible to a cop last night, aren't you?" He said.

"Yes, we did," we said.

"Well, that young cop went down to the Hole after he left you and was preaching to all the guys down there. He was praying with everyone and sharing with them all night long. He was on fire for the Lord!"

The Lord really changed his life and began using him to minister to others, so that they too could experience new life in Christ. Joy filled our hearts, as we walked over to the morgue for another nightshift.

Dot Goldie

In the middle of the night, a young Jewish girl came by for coffee. She was in a tent that was set up for Jewish believers to pray for the bodies that came in.

"What do you do all night?" I asked her.

"I sing," she said.

"Would you sing for us?" I said, and she began to sing for us in Hebrew. In the darkness of the night, she sounded like an angel. It was so beautiful.

"Can I pray for you?" I asked when she finished. She nodded and so I took her hands in mine.

" God, please reveal Yourself to her as her Messiah Jesus," I prayed, and then I felt her hands pull away.

"Thank you," she said and walked away. We never saw her again. We got to know several of the detectives and policemen who were on the night shift with us. By the end of the week, we knew how they liked their coffee—made strong and black, with white sugar.

The last morning before we were to return home to Florida, we looked up at the sun, which was just coming up. It was beautiful. Five of our "regulars" were standing all huddled together in the morning sunlight. They saw that we were leaving and called out, "See you tonight!"

"No, we are leaving to go back to Florida today," I said. They all walked over to me.

"Can I do one more thing before saying goodbye?" I asked them. And almost in unison, they said, "Anything for you, Dot!"

"Can I pray for you one last time?" They immediately bowed their heads and stood in a circle with me all holding hands with each other, as I prayed for them one more time.

Jim caught the moment on camera. It is one of my most treasured photos. Here were these giants of men, all of them over six feet tall, holding my hand, a five foot nothing. The men had tears in their eyes as I commended them into Jesus' care. The sun was up and Jim's picture of us is a fond memory of what happened after 911.

God turns everything around for good. Many hearts were softened after 911 and Jesus' name was lifted up that week in New York City. We did get a chance to see some of it on the last day. We went to the Empire State Building and were ushered up to the front of the line that was waiting there. One of the men in control of the line saw our badges and sent us up front and took us all the way up to the top. When we were standing beside some folks who were looking for the "Hole," we pointed it out to them.

"Where are you from?" one of the ladies asked when she heard our accent. This opened up a beautiful conversation that led to sharing the Gospel with them, along with other bystanders. After that we went for a buggy ride around Central Park , where we saw a few skaters on the ice rink. We watched them for a while and then moved on to see the "Big Shops!" as we call them in Scotland.

The sun shined brightly on that glorious last day, and we praised the Lord, from whom all blessings flow. We left knowing that we had planted seeds wherever we went, and left the rest to Jesus.

Edi Amine

The Dictator and President of Uganda

Back in Scotland in the 60s, when I was a fairly new Christian, we had an influx of refugees come to the country. They had been put out of their country by this dictator who had done terrible things to his people.

My minister at that time was Stewart Dixon, a charismatic preacher with the Presbyterian Church of Scotland. I loved him so much. He taught us well and encouraged me to get involved in helping some of these refugees who came to our part of the country.

I didn't know much about any of what went on in Uganda, but I knew enough that these people needed Jesus in their lives to be healed and restored. I made some inquiries and found out where these people were staying. The county gave them housing, but they had no furniture. I found out that the local Dump Collectors had a warehouse that had old bits and pieces of furniture that they gave away for free to people who needed it. So I went down to investigate, and to my surprise there were some nice pieces that would fill the house of one of the families I had contacted.

I made arrangements to get the stuff from the warehouse to the family. Our local newspaper caught hold of the story and wrote an article about how I was helping this family to get settled in and how my church had come to their rescue, even though they were not of our faith.

The family was Muslim, so they were surprised that we had taken them into our hearts even though we never knew them. We told them we loved them and wanted to help in any way possible to get them settled into their new home. The lady was overcome with tears of joy.

Salim, their oldest son, could speak very good English so we communicated through him. His dad was a quiet man. Very sad that he had to leave his country where they had their own business and had been very well off. You can tell the family was well educated. The little girls were shy at first but soon came out of it when they knew we were not going to harm them. I got some toys for the girls and that made them happy. Salim had a silver radio that he had been able to take out of the country with him and that was his treasure. Once we got the house fixed up, I took them down to the government offices to get their medical cards and work papers. The old gentleman was overwhelmed by all that we, as a church, did for them. The Lord made a way for us to open up conversation about Jesus, but the old man would not listen. However, Salim did, and he was very open to the Gospel. Between Stewart talking to him and me doing my bit, Salim accepted Jesus as his Lord and Savior.

Salim came to church on a regular basis and was accepted by everyone. He enjoyed the services that he attended and began to share with his mom and sisters, who eventually accepted Jesus as their Savior. It took a while longer before the old gentleman surrendered his life over to Jesus, but he did it and now the whole family rejoiced together.

This family was in our church for quite a long time until they decided it was time for them to move. They found work in another town and a better place to live. They were very grateful to all the people who had welcomed them and helped them get over the trauma that they had been put through by the president of Uganda. We gave them a farewell party and everyone cried, but we knew Jesus would take good care of them as they started their new life with Him.

Dot Goldie

An Answer to Prayer... 28 Years Later

My sister-in-law Mavis is like a sister to me, and one of the sweetest people you could ever meet. We have been friends ever since my brother Harris married her 50 years ago. Mavis was curious about Christianity for several years but would never commit to Jesus Christ as her Lord and Savior.

    I prayed for her continuously until one day she surrendered all to Him. Today, Mavis is in love with Jesus, and it shows! She has a kind heart and there is nothing she wouldn't do to help others. She attended a tiny little church in her village, which was filled mostly with elderly people. A perfect place for her to show her gift of hospitality, some may say.

    Mavis was made an elder in this church and served well until the Lord moved her away to another church a few years later. Looking back, it's so great to see how God had special plans for her.

    Jim and I were staying with my brother and Mavis one weekend, as Jim was doing some remodeling in their house.

Enriched by Him

One morning I was on my knees praying when Mavis came into the room.

"Oh! I'm sorry," she said and left the room.

When I went into the kitchen later on she started to ask me questions about my faith.

"Would you like to invite Jesus into your life?" I asked her after I had told her about Him.

She refused.

"I could ask Him into my life and you wouldn't know it," she said flippantly.

"Oh, yes I would," I replied.

"How would you know?" she asked.

"You would want to tell others what Jesus has done for you," I said. "You wouldn't be able to keep it to herself."

She still refused to accept Jesus so I left it alone. Only the Holy Spirit can convict a person to change, so instead of keeping on at her I decided to pray for her… for twenty-eight years!

A lot of water had gone under the bridge, as we say in Scotland, since that day in her little cottage in Scotland. But I know this, in God's time, He makes all things beautiful and that is exactly what He did in Mavis' life. I remember it well. Jim and I had moved to Florida, and Mavis and Harris came for a visit one summer. They stayed with us for a while and when they wanted to stay longer they rented a trailer, where they lived during the rest of their stay in the States. They loved it. Harris bought an old car to drive around, especially to his favorite spot: the track at Pompano Beach. He met some of the horse owners there and became friends with many of them. Harris was a horse owner himself. So he felt at home in this place.

At this time, Mavis wanted to join me at work at Riverside Christian Fellowship, where I served as the Outreach Director. She came with me on my outreach runs, including a place called Hamondville in the projects. There were a lot of homeless people who lived on the streets and slept in the bushes. There were prostitutes and pimps and junkies, and some drunks that all hung out there.

I brought them bread, cakes, and doughnuts from Publix and Dunkin Doughnuts that had been donated to our ministry. Every day they would give me their day's old goods that they couldn't sell to the public but was still good enough to eat.

The drunks only took the sweet stuff. They never wanted the bread. I took my guitar to sing to them, then shared God's Word with them before I gave out the goodies. Many of them befriended me and were my protectors. It was not the safest place in the world to be for a little five-foot tall Scottish red

Enriched by Him

head. Reportedly, many people were killed or stabbed around this place and a lot of gangs were there too, as well as drug dealers. But honestly, I never felt fear there. Jesus was with me, and I was doing His work amongst those poor lost souls.

One day during one of these runs, Mavis turned to me as we pulled into my driveway. "Dot, how do I get Jesus into my life?" She asked. "I want to be like you!"

We sat in the car for a while and I shared the Gospel with her as I had done for 28 years. The difference was this time she was ready to listen. God had been at work in her heart. Finally, I led her in a prayer where she asked Jesus to be her Lord and Savior. She cried tears of joy, and so did I.

Since that day, Mavis never looked back. After she returned to Glasgow, Scotland, she began working in a soup kitchen a couple of days a week, feeding and serving the homeless and poor people in that area, and volunteered at the local Cancer Shop twice a week for a couple of hours.

Mavis' life is so full now. She has many stories of what Jesus is doing through her these days. God is so good.

"I wish I would have asked Jesus into my life that morning when I walked into your room and saw you on your knees praying," she said. Little did she know that I had been praying for her that day. The Lord is so faithful to answer our prayers when they are offered up in faith. In Matthew 7:7 we read, *"Ask and it will be given to you; seek and you will find; knock and the door will be opened to you."*

God's Word gives us the assurance that when we pray, believing that we have received, we will. I did that and He answered me.

So, pray don't give up on praying for the ones you love. God will, in His time, do a beautiful thing in the lives of those you are praying for. Something else happens when you believe. You receive more than you asked for. In this case, my brother Harris also accepted the Lord into his life during the time they were with us in Florida.

Harris and I had gone to the Pompano Race Track, where I also had a Bible study on a day the track called the "dark night," because they did not have any racing going on.

Harris and I used to work together in our butcher shop in Scotland, where we also owned a couple of trotting horses. Harris trained them every day after work and I raced them. We had always been very close, and so when he came to visit me in Florida, I took him to the track and introduced him to many of the horse owners. He immediately became friends with them and began to go to the track every day to help out. Harris had always loved horses and knew so much about them. What he didn't know about horses was not worth knowing about! I called him a "Horse Whisperer" before that name was made famous by a movie that came out years later. He was a valuable asset to a couple of ladies that had been having trouble getting one of their horses qualified to run in a race. Harris fixed the feet of the horse and it not only qualified, but actually won the race.

Harris went to the Bible study at the track on one of those "dark nights," and another preacher came to share the Word. After the study, the preacher prayed and asked that if there was anyone who wished to receive Jesus as their Savior to raise their head. Harris lifted his head in acknowledgement that he wanted to invite Jesus into his life. That night I could hardly contain myself. I was overcome with joy. God was saving my family one by one.

When Harris and Mavis returned home to Scotland, they opened up their home for a Bible study, and for missionaries who came from the United States. For several years, missionaries from all across the States found hospitality in that little cottage. They did this for many years until Harris took ill and Mavis needed to take care of him around the clock. He was now her mission field. She did this right up until the day he died. It was a heartbreaking time for her, as she had watched him grow wearier every day. She prayed that God would take him in his sleep. And that's exactly how it happened. She kissed him goodnight one day and went to bed, and the next morning he was gone.

The funeral was a celebration, and many of Harris's unsaved friends were there. Pastor Tom asked me to give a word of testimony, and at first I was a bit chocked up, but then I regained my composure and began to share how Harris had accepted the Lord into his heart at Pompano Beach Race Track in the States. Many of the men there knew about Pompano Beach Track, for some of them had raced horses there or had visited the place while on vacation.

"If any of you wants to see Harris again, you need to surrender your lives over to Christ," I told them after I shared the Gospel with them.

Later that day, we had a dinner at the church where again people were asked to share something about Harris. The room was packed with all the trotting men and women, with whom I had grown up.

They all knew me, but they didn't know the new me. I shared my heart out at that dinner, and the church people who were serving the dinner stood by the kitchen door listening and smiling, as if to say: "Keep going, Dot!"

I was bold and they loved it.

Enriched by Him

"That was awesome to hear what God has done in your life, Dot," someone said while others told me that they wished they could share their testimonies as boldly as I had. I reminded them in a gentle way that the boldness came from Christ, not me.

Later on, a friend of mine whom I had known for years invited a group of us to dinner. She wanted to hear more about the Gospel. Again, we shared and answered many questions that night, and although no one received Jesus as their Lord and Savior, many seeds were planted. One day I pray they will bear much fruit. To the glory of God. Amen.

Fredericka and Mamma Kat

Fredericka is a beautiful black woman. She came into my office one day in need of some food from our church pantry. I listened to her story and got her to fill out some paperwork that we used to keep track of who and what they received.

Fredericka went over to the pantry, and just then I heard the Lord speaking to my heart: "Give this woman whatever she needs," He said. "I am going to bless you through her."

"If you need anymore food, come to me and I will help you, okay?" I said to her as we walked toward her car with the bags of food.

"Thank you so much, my momma will be so happy!" She said smiling a big toothless smile that lit up her whole face. When we reached her car there was a four-year old boy sitting there patiently waiting for her.

"Who are you, smiler?" I asked him, as he had the biggest smile on his chubby face.

"He is my sister's boy," Fredericka said. "She is in prison so

Enriched by Him

I'm looking after him, as well as her five other kids. My mom helps me look after the older ones."

"Can I come visit your mom?" I asked, looking to see if there was anything else we could do to help this family. Before Fredericka drove off, I shared the Gospel with her.

"My momma is a Christian, so if you want to come to the house, you are welcome," she said as she was leaving. We scheduled a time for me to go down to the house the next day, where I was welcomed with open arms and a big hug.

"Momma Kat is my name," a thin woman said. "You are welcome in my home anytime." The house was small but you could feel the love in it. Kat and I had a lovely time together sharing Jesus with one another that afternoon.

"Would you like to start a Bible study in your home?" I said.

"Praise the Lord! I would be honored," said Kat, who told me about "The Hole and The Ugly Corner," where the homeless lived and hung out.

Fredericka turned out to be the one who came with me to give out the food there. God had told me to sign her up as an assistant for the outreach to the homeless and the down and outs in Hammondville. Soon thereafter, we started the Bible study at Kat's house. She invited neighbors to come and hear, and her other daughter Frankie, who was a deaconess at their church, came also. I invited some of my team to come as well and we had a great time sharing and singing praises to God. One of Kat's neighbors wanted to come but couldn't because she was bedridden. So we took the meeting to her for about an hour then went back to Kat's house, where the rest of the neighbors had gathered. We did this for several years; it was such a blessing.

Fredericka invited Jesus into her life very soon after we started the Bible study at Kat's house. I had the privilege of leading her to the Throne of Grace, where she gave her heart to the Lord. She was baptized in our church a week later.

Fredericka shared her testimony. "When I came to your church for help, I knew something was different about Dot," she said. "She accepted me as I was. I felt loved for the first time in my life."

She told us about a woman she witnessed to the day before her baptism. This woman was an old enemy of Fredericka's. She'd had many fights in the past with her, and now this woman wanted to fight her over her newfound faith.

"She lunged at me but the Lord restrained me from fighting back," said Fredericka, who recounted how the woman had clawed at her neck and face, and yelled names at her, then left.

The congregation was amazed at her testimony, and so was

Enriched by Him

I. She was a new creation in Christ. The old was gone, and the new had come. Praise the Lord! We saw many people come to Christ, as well as many healings take place at Kat's place. One Haitian woman came with her little baby who was very sick. We prayed for him and we saw the change take place in him as we prayed. The woman was praying and crying at the same time as she saw the scars on little Andrew begin to disappear before her eyes. She took all the bandages off that were on him and as she unwrapped him, his little body was completely healed.

"I have never seen an instant healing before," said one of my team members, who was shaking like a leaf. We all praised God that day. It was a blessing for all who were there.

The word soon spread and many more came to the house the following Tuesday morning. A man who was blind was brought by some of the guys at the Ugly Corner. We prayed for him but nothing happened. Then, we began to praise the Lord.

"Something's going on in my eye," he suddenly said, and we continued to pray. Nothing happened. I could tell that it was a bit disappointing for those who were looking for another miracle to happen.

"The rest is up to you, Lord," I prayed and left it in His hands.

The next time we went down to Kat's I saw the man who we had prayed for. I was driving into the street and he waved at me. He could see! He told us later at the meeting that as he walked home that day, the Lord had healed him. What a Savior! God met that man's needs at the right time. You know, we don't deserve anything from God, but in His mercy He still delivers His goodness. So, wait expectantly and receive His best.

This reminds me of a passage of Scripture I hope you can meditate on, one that clearly communicates what God does for us when we are willing to believe in Him.

"And therefore the Lord waits to be gracious to you; and therefore He lifts Himself up, that He may have mercy on you and show loving-kindness to you. For the Lord is a God of justice. Blessed are all those who wait for Him, who expect and look and long for Him!" Isaiah 30:18.

Kat's little house became a safe haven for many people in that bad area. Kat kept her door open for anyone who had a need, and as a result, all kinds of people came. Like in the days of the early church, we saw the sick, the lame, the blind, and the needy come and hear the Word of God.

Tuesday's at Kat's was a highlight of the community. As many as twenty people worshipped the Lord and heard the Word, and as passers by stopped by the doorstep to listen, we would invite them to come in. The Bible was not all we taught. A few schoolteachers joined us during the summer to help us teach

Enriched by Him

kids and adults to read and write. I have a short video that was made during that time showing a nineteen-year old boy holding up his A B C's that he had been learning. He wrote his name for the first time as well. It was a glorious time. God was showing Himself to these poor souls and they absolutely loved Him.

Many other wonderful things happened there and over at the Ugly corner. We helped an old man who lived in a little room that was rat infested. We took a team down there one Saturday morning and gutted the whole place and disinfected everything. Jim hauled away a truckload of junk that was the man's furniture and replaced it with some things that Jim built for him. The old man was so happy we had done this for him. He had two pictures that he wanted hung up on the wall. One was of his mother and the other one was of me! While we were cleaning, a car pulled up outside and a big guy got out and asked me what the @#$#% we were doing.

"We are just fixing the place up to make it fit for humans to live in," I said. The guy had been sent by the owner who had eyes everywhere, especially on us. I guess he thought we were from the Health Department. "You should be ashamed taking 300 dollars a month from this old man to live in a rat hole like this!" I told the guy. He got back in his car and drove away in a hurry. We never saw him again.

Dot Goldie

One day a mother of a teenage girl approached me. She said, "Can you help me get my daughter back?" She asked.

"Back from where?" I said.

"She is in the crack house," she said, describing a white painted, broken down building in the back of the Hole. The mother was afraid to go there by herself so she asked me to go with her.

"Let's pray before we go in," I told her. "I just want Jesus and a few of His angels to go before us, okay?" She nodded, so we prayed, and on our way we went.

The door was unlocked. So, we went in.

There were no lights, only darkness. An awful smell filled our nostrils as we walked in and almost collided with the bodies that laid all over the floor. It looked like a CSI-worthy crime scene or a Sci-fi film. From the little we could see, drugs were not only legal in this place, it was plentiful. And it seemed to be managed by very unsavory underworld characters, who were not people to be trifled with by the regular citizenry.

"Which one is your daughter?" I asked the mom. She spotted her in a corner all huddled up in a ball holding her legs tight to her body. The girl was stoned out of her mind. She didn't know where she was or who we were. Somehow, we managed to get her up on her feet and as we were almost to the

Enriched by Him

door a big guy came in. "What are you doing?" He said, not very politely, but I'll skip the extra words.

"We're taking her home," I said very boldly.

"You better not take any of my stuff!" He said, like a bad character you might find behind the scenes into the seamy side of a city.

"You have nothing that we want," I said and walked out the door, forgetting all the bodies and the evidence of a crime. Our focus was only on the one girl, but it broke my heart to leave the others behind. Such drug availability is a large part of the appeal of a crack house to high school and college age kids today. It doesn't matter what part of town they come from, they know they can find that drugs are plentiful there and they ignore the danger and the darkness behind those walls.

We got into the van and I drove the girl right down to the rehab center that I had visited with some other people. They admitted her right away. The mom was in tears.

"Thank you, Jesus!" The mom cried over and over.

She had no idea that I had been shaking like a leaf during the whole time we were in that crack house and the confrontation with that big guy. The reality is we may never know how dangerous the situation really was, but we do know that the Lord protected and upheld me on that day and the many years I worked in that area of town. The "crack house" it's probably still there, because the drug people are forever confident that if anyone searches for them, they will always produce what they want. In their minds, "forever" is timeless, and their crimes is like an unsolved mystery.

Fredericka was diagnosed with breast cancer years later, and was admitted to the hospital, where she had her breast removed. Our church provided a prosthetic breast for her and she recovered very quickly. She later resumed working with us for many years until I left.

That's about the time when the Lord led Jim and I to serve at Calvary Chapel Fort Lauderdale. Fredericka carried on the work for a while after I left but then Kat took ill and she left to take care of her. Kat died shortly after that and I was invited to the funeral. It was a great day as we celebrated another saint taking residence up in heaven. We imagined the angels singing and rejoicing, while down here on earth, it seemed like the whole of Hammonville had turned out for the celebration. Momma Kat was greatly loved by all these people. The service lasted about three hours. One by one, people got up to say how Momma Kat had helped them, or fed them, or looked after their babies. It was a tearjerker. She was greatly missed by all.

A Weekend at Fort Meyers Beach

Jim and I celebrated our 48th Wedding Anniversary on July 18, 2012. Just before that, we had hosted a three-day missions retreat, and I had cooked three meals a day for more than 60 missionaries and their kids. While I did have some help from a few girls, who did some prep work, I did the bulk of the cooking.

The day after the retreat ended, I was more than ready for a retreat of my own. Jim and I set off for Fort Meyers Beach. I stretched out in the seat of the car, closed my eyes and before I knew it I heard Jim say, "We're here!"

I sat up in my seat and there before me was the beautiful blue water and sandy beach, waiting for us! We checked in and found our room, which was right on the beach. Just beautiful! We immediately unpacked, found our swim suits and towels and went down to the beach to gaze at the beauty of that glorious, peaceful sea.

There was hardly anyone out there. It seemed as if God had set aside this wee part of the beach just for us. We pulled up a couple of beach chairs and sat there in perfect harmony. The lapping of the waves was like a lullaby, and so I closed my eyes.

"Thank you, Jesus for this place, and my darling husband for thinking about doing such a lovely thing for me after working so hard the past three days," I prayed silently. "Thank you, Lord for my Jim. Please bless him for his thoughtfulness."

We sat there for over an hour before we got up to go get ready for something to eat. It was so relaxing just to flip off my shoes and sink my feet into the sand and let it run through my toes. I really felt like I was on vacation now.

We went back to our room and got dressed to go to dinner. We strolled around the hotel for a wee while and then went into the restaurant overlooking the water. It was nice and cool, and a gentle breeze floated over us as we sat there listening to the music playing. We ordered our meal and relaxed, chatting away as we ate. I was glad I did not have to make the meal this time!

By now the place was beginning to get busy and people were talking loud over the music, so when we finished eating we escaped back to the hotel room for a while.

"Would you like to go for a swim in the pool?" I suggested to Jim.

"Nah, but I'll go with you," he said. So I got ready and we went over to the pool. There were a lot of people there all sitting on the edges and kids jumping in and having a blast. Jim sat down on a deck chair and took hold of my watch, and as he took it from me, he drew me in and gave me a kiss on the cheek.

"Go have fun!" He said, and so I went in. I didn't jump in, because I'm scared to go under, which it's funny, really. Because the way Jim describes me, is someone who jumps into the ocean head on, while he is the kind who likes to go and get a raft with a safety vest, ensuring that he will not drown if possible.

I stepped into the pool and there was a little girl with her grandparents playing beside me. We chatted and asked where each of us was from.

"Are you a Christian?" The woman suddenly asked, to my surprise.

"I am," I said.

"I just told my husband, 'these two people are Christians,'" she said as she noticed the love of Jesus in Jim as he treated me, as we settled down on the beach chairs.

It just goes to show you, people are watching you and you don't even know it. Praise God we were a good witness and that these people saw Jesus in us. This couple was from up north and had come for a vacation to see their granddaughter. Their daughter was going through a divorce and they wanted to give the little one a vacation before the parents split.

Dot Goldie

We took the opportunity to pray for them right there at the pool. They were very appreciative for the prayer and thanked us very much. They asked where we worshipped and we told them Calvary Chapel Fort Lauderdale. Their faces lit up at this.

"We go to Calvary Chapel in Philly!" the woman said and we became instant friends. It always amazes me when Christians meet for the first time, and then you end up as if you had known each other all your life.

"Are you from Glasgow, Scotland?" the woman asked.

"Yes, we are!" I said. She had recognized my accent as being from Glasgow, as her best friend was from there and she I sounded just like her.

I prayed and said, "Thank you, Lord for new friends in you. I know we will see them soon when you return!"

Enriched by Him

First Class with Jesus

One time, during our way back to Hungary in the mission field, after our time at home with the family, we set off for the airport with plenty of time to spare. We got our luggage, checked in, and got our tickets.

We were all set, or so we thought.

We boarded the plane on time. Everyone was seated with their seat belts fastened and settled in for the flight.

Then it happened.

The captain came over the speaker and informed us that we were being delayed because of bad weather in New York. JFK had told them that there was a lightening storm there and they wanted us to wait till it passed, then we could take off. We sat on the plane and waited. We were told it would be fifteen minutes then we could go.

Wrong.

The captain then came back on and said if we wanted to we could deplane, but warned us not to go too far away because we could leave pretty soon. So some people got off, but Jim and I decided to stay on board and wait. We chatted with some of the passengers to pass the time. The crew came around with water for us to drink while we waited. Then the captain came out and chatted with Jim and me about the situation at JFK. He was a very nice guy and answered all our questions.

"You can still make it on time to get your connection to Budapest," he said. So we were confident that as he was the captain he could do it.

Well, time passed and we still did not take off. Then came the shocking news. It would be three hours before we could take off. The crew served us lunch while we waited. Eventually the call was made for the passengers who had deplaned to come back on board. They all got settled in and we were off. According to the captain, we still had time to make it to Budapest, so we sat back and relaxed.

Finally, the announcement came over the speaker that we were about to land. Everyone fasted up their seat belts and put their seat backs up straight and waited for the landing.

Then it happened again.

The captain informed us that he could not land right away because he didn't have a parking spot. A parking spot?

What was this, Walmart?

Enriched by Him

We circled around the airport for another fifteen minutes. Now Jim and I were really worried about our connecting flight to Budapest. We finally landed and we tried to get past some people to get off the plane so we could get our connection. People understood and tried their best to let us pass but in the end we had to wait our turn. When we got off we had to collect our bags and get them moved to another place. We saw our cases and tried to reach them, when we were told by the airline staff to leave them there.

They were very rude to us. Jim tried to speak kindly to the woman at the desk and she would not even look up at him.

"We need tickets for Budapest so that we can still catch our flight," Jim said.

"You will have to wait over there!" She said without even looking at him. Instead, she pointd to another spot where luggage was being transferred.

A man behind us got really angry and a few others joined in. This woman ignored all of us and could not care less whether or not we got to our destinations or not. The place was in an uproar now.

"Where are your bags?" A small boy asked and we showed him. He promptly put them onto the right track for Budapest. We were ushered into an area where everyone who missed a flight were to line up and get new tickets. By this time, Jim was not feeling well. He is diabetic and he really needed something to eat. So I tried to find a chocolate bar, which he ate but still did not feel well. I told him to lie down on the bench and I would go and get the tickets. I waited in line with all the other people, and eventually it was my turn. I gave the young man my information, and he looked up at me with eyes that said its own story before it was told.

"I am sorry, Madam, but the flight you were booked on has left and there won't be another one until 9 P.M. tomorrow evening," he said.

I burst into tears. We were both exhausted with all the things that had taken place earlier. And now, Jim needed food and there was nothing available, only sweets.

"I am so sorry, let me see what I can do," the young man said, as he tried to get us on the next flight even though it was fully booked.

I joked with him and said, "I'll take two first class tickets, please," and smiled at him.

"Please take a seat Madam, and wait with your husband. I'll get back to you," he said. All the personnel were on break. Sure enough a while later the young man came back and walked over to us and handed me the tickets.

Enriched by Him

"Madam, I am sorry you have had such a bad experience with us. I hope this will ease the pain you have been through," he said and handed me two first class tickets all the way to Budapest.

He personally escorted us to another place. "Food will be available through here, but remember, once you go through customs you can not come out again," he said.

We nodded and went with him. It was so quiet back there. No one was being checked, only Jim and me. All the other people had to wait out amongst the crowds. The customs people could not have been nicer to us. In fact, they treated us like royalty.

"Have a good night," they said as they pointed where the food court and the restrooms were in the waiting area. The treatment was unreal after all we had been through.

"I wish you a safe journey home to Budapest," said the young man who had given us the tickets.

"Can I pray for you?" I asked him.

"Yes, please!" He said.

"Thank you, Lord Jesus, for this young man's kindness toward Jim and me. Please Jesus, bless him for all he has done in going out of his way to see that we got fixed up with all our needs," I prayed.

Dot Goldie

"Thank you so much for your prayer," he said. He had noticed that we were Christians and saw that we were both a bit older and had been harassed by some attendants at the arrival place. "I am so sorry for their behavior," he said before turning and walking away.

I got some hot food for the both of us and then sat down in peace and quiet to enjoy our meal together. After eating, we looked around for a place to lie down and sleep for the night. By this time it was around two in the morning. I saw a couple of quilts laying on the floor that someone must have brought off the plane from First Class. I picked them up and brought them over to Jim. No one else was there. *This is God's supply for my needs*, I thought.

We curled up on the floor and tried to sleep. It was a restless night. I was up and down trying to get comfy, but the hard floor was relentless. It was a rough night. In the morning we found ourselves next to another older couple.

"What are your flight plans?" They asked. And as it turned out, they had been delayed and had missed their connecting flights too. We chatted for a while and during our conversation we found out that they were retired missionaries.

"We are missionaries too!" We told them, and that started a whole new conversation about what Jesus was doing in our lives. It was so nice. We had breakfast together and walked around with them during the day until their flight was called. They left us around three or four in the afternoon. We marveled at how God was working in all of this. That which the devil meant for evil, God turned around for good.

Praise His Name!

After walking around and going for more food, the time went by quite quickly and before we knew it we were boarding our plane for Budapest.

First Class really is FIRST CLASS. We were offered drinks before we were even in our seats. We had some orange juice and sat back to enjoy our flight. Then the attendant approached us and handed us a menu.

"What would you like for dinner?" She asked. We were amazed! We had real stainless steel cutlery, clothl napkins, big pillows and nice quilts, like the ones we had found at the airport. It was so different from what we were used to having.

I know you are all dying to know what was on the menu, right? Filet steak, soup, salad, and a nice dessert—all on real plates and real cups and saucers for our tea. The service on that flight was wonderful. We stretched out on our bed seats and watched our own little TV set. We soon fell asleep.

We were awakened by the steward asking us, "What would

you like for breakfast?" She handed us a menu to choose from, and all was delicious. Soon it was time to get ready for landing. The steward helped me with my tray. I couldn't get it in the slot by the side of my chair. I think he knew we were not "first class flying type of people!"

The flight was over and we were out on the airport waiting for our ride back home to Vajta. One of our very dear brothers in the Lord came smiling in the doors looking for us. He saw us and came over and hugged us as if we had been gone forever.

He had missed us! He picked up our bags like they were nothing and loaded them onto a cart and wheeled us all out of there to the car waiting outside.

He wanted to know blow by blow how things went on our trip. So, we related the whole story to him on the two-hour drive back to the castle in Vajta.

"I'm jealous," he said when we told him the bit about the first class seats, but he was happy for us that it all had worked out well in the end.

God has a way of doing that, doesn't He? I love Him so very much for all His goodness toward us, His children. Odd and frustrating things happen in life and we don't understand them at the time. But God, in His wisdom, knows what the plans are for His people. We were blessed so much after all the turmoil we

Enriched by Him

went through at that airport.

Looking back on it all, I praise God for every moment that we had. It gave us a great God story to tell others about how God does turn everything around for the good for those who love him. Amen?

Jesus Said to me,

"Walk in the Garden with Me"

"Lord, please speak to me," I asked the Lord as I was walking in the garden at the castle in Vajta one morning. I enjoyed the peace and quiet, and the particularly inviting scenery, which was hilly in some places and flat in other spots. Calvary Chapel had brought back the castle to its orginal beauty. It had once belonged to someone of prominence, but it now served the sons and daughters of the Lord of Lords, and King of Kings, Jesus Christ!

Aside from basking in the beauty of the picturesque surroundings, it was really good exercise, if you like that kind of thing. I've always loved walking in the early hours before it gets too busy, and my thoughts don't get interrupted by other things. So, on this day, I arrived at my favorite viewing spot and smiled. There, in front of me I could see the fields for miles. Colors of yellow, tans, browns and green dressed the horizon, with sunflowers blooming in the distance all the way to the

Enriched by Him

next village. Immediately, peace engulfed me as I sat there, overlooking this amazing view. As I praised the Lord, He began to speak into my heart.

"*Listen,*" He said. So I listened to the sounds of birds singing their praises to the Lord. I continued to listen and heard the bees buzzing around and the wafting of the trees in the breeze. It was so peaceful I just wanted this to last forever and not change. The sky was a pale blue with puffy white clouds moving slowly across the sky. It felt like heaven to me just sitting there.

As I sat, I glanced down on the bench seat. There were two tiny snails sitting right beside me. One of them was rolled up in a tight, little ball, while the other one had his head popped out. As I went to touch it, the snail pulled his head back inside his shell to protect himself. Then the Lord spoke to me.

"*I am your protection against any trouble that comes your way,*" He said and I looked over at the little snail and his protective shell. As I lingered there, I thanked the Lord for all his mercies that are new every morning and for His goodness and protection and most of all, for His agape love for me. I closed my eyes for a few seconds, perhaps minutes, I don't know.

Suddenly, I felt His presence all around me, and the quiet was interrupted by His soft voice saying: "*Walk with me in the Garden.*"

Dot Goldie

I got up and began walking. I looked down on the field below me where there was a huge hedge cut out in the shape of a cross. As I approached the rough and unsteady broken steps that led down to the cross, the voice inside me again spoke in quiet tones.

"*The road I walked to the cross was painful and rough for me, and at times it will be for you also. You will have painful times in your life but go through the cross,*" He said.

As I walked through the middle of the cross on the field, the ground beneath my feet was flat and easy to walk on. As I continued my walk, I came out of the shade of the cross and into the sunshine.

The Lord said, "*Walk through the light.*" The sun was now shining beyond the cross, which was now behind me in the shade. As I reached the end of the cross (it is a huge big cross just so you know!), I looked back up toward the castle and the sun shone brightly above it.

The Lord said to me, "*Gaze at it. Now that you have come through the cross, you are now in the light.*"

I was filled with joy at this thought. *I am going to spend eternity walking in the light of Jesus, my Savior and LORD.*

What a blessed thought! As I traveled along the grounds, I walked into the shade of some beautiful trees that lined the pathway back toward the castle. And again I heard the voice saying, *"I am still here walking with you."* As if to say, "I will never leave you or forsake you in the dark and shaded times of your life."

I came back into the sunshine again and into the light, and once more the voice inside me said, as I saw my shadow in front of me, *"I go before you."*

As my shadow was by my side, I heard the voice saying, *"I am with you every step you take."* When my shadow was behind me, I heard His voice saying, *"I will guard you from behind and give my angels charge over you."*

It was awesome how this all took place. I ended back up on the bench where the converstion started, and would you believe the two little snails were still there? The same snail had his head popped out again until I touched the bench with my water bottle, and he pulled it right back into the shell, still afraid of anything bigger than him.

Then Jesus said to me, *"You don't have to fear anything, for I am with you wherever you go. You are more than a conqueror in Me."*

I thanked the Lord for our walk together around the garden and rose up from the bench. I took a drink of water from my bottle, and then He said to me: *"Drink in the living water daily* and I will fill you to overflowing. You will not be able to contain it. Out of you will flow rivers of living water to quench the thirst of those thirsty souls I will send to you. You will teach them how to drink for themselves and they will never thirst again for they will be taught by Me, through you, to come to the water and be cleansed and fed and set free!"

I finished my walk in the sunshine of His smile. I felt so refreshed and radiant. I had to write it all down as soon as I got inside my house so that I would not forget what happened on my walk in the garden with my Lord and Savior, Jesus.

Praise His holy name!

The Children of Honduras

Jim and I have done several short mission trips during our walk with the Lord. They all have been special and this one to Honduras was no exception. Actually, it was truly a heartbreaker.

We went to a small and run down orphanage called El Parisio. They hardly had any food, only rice, and they cooked that on a little round mound of a clay oven that was made to perform like a stovetop and an oven.

The children had no extra clothes or shoes, and some even didn't have any at all. Their beds were strips of wood on a bare floor with hardly any sheets or blankets or pillows. Even in such poverty, I have never seen such happy kids. They smiled the whole time we were there.

We had brought clothes and shoes with us that our church had donated, along with some toys for the little ones. My friend Norma and her husband Orlando are Spanish and know the language very well. They told the kids we had new clothes and shoes and some toys for them.

Dot Goldie

"Sit on the benches and we will come by and fit you with shoes," they told the kids. "Then you can pick out what clothes you would like."

They all sat down, smiles all around. Eyes wide open waiting and watching. Norma gave out the shoes. Some were looking a little concerned as they watched and wondered if there were going to be any left to go around for all of them. In reality there was an abundance of shoes that would be there when they grew out of the ones they had picked out; the same went for the clothes. God provided bountifully for these little ones and the ladies who took care of them.

One little girl, about four-years old, picked out a pair of shoes for herself and put them on. Her little face lit up with the biggest smile you ever saw! She had been sitting waiting her turn and had no smile at all but when Norma fitted the shoes on her, her whole face changed completely. However, when she went to walk in them she was limping a little. The shoes were too small for her.

Norma explained that we could give her another pair that wouldn't hurt her toes. But she would not part with them. Eventually she gave in and tried on another pair and this time they fitted her perfectly. Her face beaming, she went dancing all over the little compound where we were sitting.

Enriched by Him

Then there was this boy. He was about eleven years old. He had a cheeky face. He was like something out of a Charles Dickens story—a scamp of a boy but happy as a lark. Guess what he picked out for a T-shirt?

A luminous pink T-shirt with the picture of a black silhouette of an old fashioned lady wearing a hat with a feather in it! It was hilarious. He pranced around in that thing all day after putting it on. There was no way he was going to part with that T-shirt. We all laughed so hard our tummies ached. He did get some other things but his pink T-shirt was his pride and joy. I can still see him in my mind's eye as he danced around with that toothy smile on his face wearing that "ridiculous" T-shirt!

All the kids and workers got new clothes and shoes that day. Everyone was happy to say the least. We also filled their pantry with food and bought them a new stove so that they could cook without having to build a fire under the clay oven. We bought pots and pans as well so their kitchen was stocked with everything they would need.

In return, we were blessed beyond measure with all the smiles and hugs we got from those beautiful children. We also gave the pastor who oversees the orphanage one of the vans I used for my outreach ministry. We got it shipped out to him before our arrival, and he was overcome with joy.

Dot Goldie

He could now go and pick up the village people in the mountains and bring them to church each night. Yes, you read right. There's church every night there, including Sundays.

This pastor was also the worship leader. He led with his trumpet as the choir sang the songs, then he preached the Word with passion and boldness.

The actual church building was four pillars, all open to the weather with low wooden benches on the dirt floor. But oh, how these people loved the Lord and praised Him for all that they had. They really put us all to shame. They were so filled with the joy of the Lord and continued to praise Him for all His goodness to them. I will never forget my time there. It surely was an eye opener for me. El Paraiso will be etched in my heart forever.

Enriched by Him

The Fields of Heaven

The beauty of this life

Is but a fragrance of the fields of Heaven

The bird on the wing

The snowflakes on the trees

The sounds of streams

All such as these are but the first notes of the eternal song

To Sister Dot,

With love,

Brother Peter

This is a poem that my friend Peter Waugh wrote to me many years ago while sitting in St. Giles Cathedral in Edinburgh. It is called "The Fields of Heaven." Peter wrote it on the backside of a form we used in the Church of Scotland for the youth group that we used to lead together. I have kept it for more than forty years. It is tattered and torn now and stuck together with tape, but I will never part with it.

Dot Goldie

Peter and his wife Margaret are our daughter's godparents. They have been our dearest friends since we first met. Even though we don't see each other very often, when we do meet, it is as if we have never been apart. We always find something to laugh about. We enjoy recounting the days when we were growing up in the Lord together in the Church of Scotland.

Peter had quite the sense of humor. He used to call the old ladies who came to the church dressed in their fur coats the *Fur Coat Brigade*. One time we invited the street gangs to come into church and these old ladies moved away to the other side of the church, not wanting to sit beside them. They were a bit stuffy, but I suppose they were also a bit afraid of them too!

Peter could always see humor in things that were stuffy and make a joke of it, and we would laugh until our sides hurt. We shared some wonderful times together as couples and with all our children during the summer holidays. We would all go to our caravan in North Berwick in Scotland, where the children would enjoy a time at the beach, even though it was freezing cold sometimes. We also did what we called Summer Mission.

The Church of Scotland would have these beach missions and evangelize the folks sitting on the beach. We would gather a crowd around and sing songs of praise and then someone would give a testimony, and the Word would be preached with boldness. I loved these old days. One time standing in the pouring rain the minister asked me, "Why are you here?"

"To share the Gospel of Jesus Christ with anyone who may listen and wants their lives changed as Jesus has changed mine," I replied.

Many people gave their hearts to Christ that night. A few even came back with us to the church to talk and learn more about Jesus. It was amazing to see people standing in the rain, listening to God's Word, like in that scene in *Chariots of Fire*, where Eric Liddell is standing at a race track in the pouring rain under an umbrella, sharing the Gospel with a crowd of men. They all hung onto his every word, and as he finished speaking the sun came out.

That night at the church, the Son came out and changed many lives, who had been waiting for such a time as this. Those were the days when we were young and could stay up all night talking, and never get tired. I am old now, but the Gospel never gets old. There is always something new every day when I read it with a heart full of expectation, and the Lord never disappoints me.

I love him so much! I pray He gives me more of His Spirit and His words so that I may share it with whoever will listen.

Praying for a Donkey

One day, when I was a new Christian, I was visiting my parents and my brother Harris, who lived next door to them. He had a cute little donkey called Jenny. Growing up in my family, we always had horses and a donkey. Well, on this particular day, Jenny was not feeling well and my brother was quite worried about her.

Jenny used to roam around the grounds and if you left the kitchen door open she would walk right in. She was like a pet to all of us and all the kids in the neighborhood loved her. But that day she was laying down in the front yard with her head down.

This was not a good sign.

Harris came into my mom's house and said, "I'm calling the vet," and that was definitely not a good sign, for there was nothing Harris couldn't do for a horse. But, on that day he was stumped. As he explained the situation to us, we all started crying.

"Let me pray over her," I said.

Harris just looked at me and said, "Just stay inside."

Enriched by Him

At first, I did stay inside and watched Harris try to keep Jenny's head up. Thoughts were running through my mind about how Jesus healed people.

Why not a wee donkey? I thought. I remembered reading John 14:12, which says, *"Most assuredly, I say to you, he who believes in Me, the works that I do he will do also; and greater works than these he will do, because I go to My Father."*

So I went outside, and asked Jesus to heal Jenny.

I felt like the Lord said, "Go lay hands on her and she will be healed."

I related the story from the Bible to Harris about how God used a donkey in Numbers 22 to talk to a man called Balaam, and how when Jesus came into Jerusalem he rode on a donkey. Harris just looked at me as though I was crazy, but I prayed anyway. I laid my hands on her head and just asked Jesus to heal this donkey that everyone loved. After I prayed I went back inside and just watched and waited to see what Jesus would do.

A half hour later, the vet arrived. And Jenny stood up just as he walked up to her. The vet examined her and couldn't find a thing wrong with her.

"Jesus healed her!" I told him, and he continued to examine her to see what had caused her to be sick.

"She's fine," he said then gave her a shot, and that was that!

Dot Goldie

From that day on, Jenny never got sick again and all the kids in the family enjoyed her for many years. Everyone wondered what had made Jenny get up all of a sudden and act as if nothing was wrong with her.

I knew who it was that made her well.

It was my awesome God who cares about everything and everyone in our lives, including a wee little donkey named Jenny.

Back then, I was a new Christian and didn't know what to do except pray. Funny thing... that's all we need to do in any season. Praise God our healer!

My Baptism in the Holy Spirit

I remember the day well. I had been at my friend's house the night before for Bible study. It was a great night as usual. I sat at the feet of John Phillips, one of the best Bible teachers ever. John walked and talked his faith every day. He was a retired coal miner but he knew the Word like no one I ever knew. I was just a baby in the Lord.

"Odd thing, sometimes I'm thinking about something and then it happens!" I told John during one of our tea breaks. "Like now… I think Mr. McGhee is coming to the study tonight."

Just as I said that, we heard a knock. Guess who was at the door? Mr. McGhee, the minister! He very seldom came to our study, but here he was.

"Isn't that weird? That's what has been happening to me lately," I told John.

As we settled back down in the living room to continue with the study, John leaned over to me and said, "Ask the Lord to baptize you in the Holy Spirit."

Dot Goldie

I looked at him and said, "Okay." I didn't know what that was, but John told me to do it so it had to be good! At the end of the night, we all said our goodbyes to each other and left.

The next morning, when I was having my quiet time with the Lord, I asked Him to baptize me in the Holy Spirit, like John said I should. I didn't know what to expect, if anything.

"Lord, please fill me with your Holy Spirit," I prayed and suddenly I heard myself saying words I had never heard before. I didn't understand. Words just kept coming to me. I began to get a bit anxious.

"Lord, if this is not from you, I don't want it!" I prayed. But the words kept on coming. I was praising the Lord in a strange language that I had never heard of before.

"This is the gift of the Holy Spirit," the Lord said. I didn't know anything about the Holy Spirit or gifts, or any of that stuff. I was just a baby Christian!

I opened up my Bible to the book of Romans and read chapters 12, 13 and 14, where it talked about the gifts. After praying and asking the Lord to give me peace about this, I felt His presence come over me like when I first got saved.

I was afraid to tell anyone what happened to me that morning. I didn't tell John, and not even Jim! For quite a long time I kept this all to myself. I felt if I told anyone they would think I was crazy. But as the Lord would have it, our group wanted to go to a conference at a place called Creif Hydro in Perth, Scotland. It was a beautiful place in the hills of Scotland, and it was there that I got relief from all my fears.

One day, one of the ministers got a word from the Lord saying that there was a woman in the congregation that was crying in her closet, and worrying about what was going on inside her.

God says, "You are mine and I love you. You are precious in my sight; the door is open to you. I love you with an everlasting love; fear not!"

Lord, if that's me, then let the next preacher say something about it, I prayed. Wouldn't you know it? Pastor Tom Smail stood up and the first thing out of his mouth was, "If that lady would like to speak to one us of later we will be happy to speak with you."

I knew then it was me. But did I go right then? No! I waited until the evening session, and at the end of the service they had a time for the laying on of hands to receive the Holy Spirit. So I stayed behind with Jim and our friends Peter, Margaret and Sheila.

Peter looked at me and said, "Dot, what you are waiting for? You have this!"

Dot Goldie

I had never said anything to him, but as the meeting was just starting, I just let it go. A few of the pastors walked around the room and laid hands on people. You could hear them begin to speak in tongues, as I had now learned that's what that was. Soon one of the pastors came to me and as he laid his hand on my head and shoulder, he looked down at me and said, "Dot, this is not what you want?"

I was shocked that he knew my name. I forgot I had a badge on my jacket with my name on it. He knelt down in front of me and said, "You are the woman we talked about this morning," he said. The tears just flowed down my face; I could not control them. God actually spoke about to me!

The pastor then proceeded to tell me everything that I had been going through to the last detail. I was amazed. How could God speak to this man and tell him all about me? I now know that is by the power of the Holy Spirit at work in those who believe.

That night I was filled afresh with the Holy Spirit and I spoke in tongues the whole night through! Jim was laughing at me, and I lit up like a Christmas tree. I was so free I didn't care what anyone thought.

Before that, the enemy had me thinking that I was a fraud. But no more. How irrational is that thinking? But alas, that's how the devil had me trapped for all these weeks. Douglas was able to break that by translating the words I spoke. It took me a while to say the words at first, but he convinced me that I would be fine. So, I let loose and a flood of words came out of my mouth, as tears flowed from my eyes.

"Well, Lord, I have never heard that language before but you know it! So, I wait for you to tell me what Dot just said," Douglas said.

Then it happened. Douglas began to interpret the words I spoke. *"My daughter, you are mine and I love you. Do not be afraid. You are mine and you are precious in My sight. The door is open to you. You belong to me. I love you, my precious child."*

It was like the message I had received that morning through Tom Smail. The burden had been lifted. The fear was gone. I was free and filled anew with the Holy Spirit. I burst into tears. The release of just knowing I was not a fraud and that God loved me was amazing. I was not crazy or anything like that. This was truly a gift from God to me—His daughter.

The next day, people were saying things like, "You got blessed last night!" or "The Shekinah Glory is all over you." That was the first time I had heard that expression. I later found out what it meant. My face was shining with God's sweet glow! It was wonderful. In fact, I felt different; it was great!

The Lord gave me a couple of words that morning. Isaiah 60:1, which says, *"Arise, shine; For your light has come! And the glory of the Lord is risen upon you."* The other one was Isaiah 61:1, which says, *"The Spirit of the Lord God is upon Me, Because the Lord has anointed Me To preach good tidings to the poor; He has sent Me to heal the brokenhearted, To proclaim liberty to the captives, And the opening of the prison to those who are bound."*

WOW! How is that for a confirmation?

I never will forget that night and following morning. I was totally set free in the Lord and have been ever since. My life has been one adventure after the other. God has blessed me in ministry, not because of anything that I can do, but by His mighty power. It's through His Spirit that we are able to do what He calls us to do, in His Name.

Glory be to God our Father and the Lord Jesus Christ, His only begotten Son.

Amen? Amen.

Shortly after that incredible encounter with the Lord, we went to another conference that taught on the Baptism in the Holy Spirit. Lord George McCloud was the main speaker. We were at our friend Sandy's church in the Kingdom of Fyffe, in Scotland.

Enriched by Him

In the morning before we left, I had my quiet time and had asked the Lord to fill me afresh with His Spirit. I was reading in Joel 2:28-29, which says, *"And it shall come to pass afterward That I will pour out My Spirit on all flesh; Your sons and your daughters shall prophesy, Your old men shall dream dreams, Your young men shall see visions. Even on my servants both men and women I will pour out my Spirit in those days."*

I left for the conference full of confidence that I would be filled again. When the service was over, Lord George made an alter call for those wishing to be filled afresh to come forward. I was the first one up there.

Lord, I'm not leaving here until you bless me! I told the Lord.

When George went to lay hands on me, I was already speaking in tongues, quietly. He looked at me and said, "You already have this, dear!"

Looking over to Sandy, who was beside him, he said, "She is already baptized."

Sandy looked on and said, "Oh, yes, she is baptized in the Spirit." But I stayed there at the steps of that alter until the Lord blessed me, and He did!

"All the gifts will flow in you at times," Lord George said. "God will use you in many ways to bring Him Glory. All you have to do is be obedient."

So, there you have it!

It was quite a journey and a very special time for me in my walk with the Lord. He continues to fill me on a daily basis, and even when I "leak," He is right there, ready to refill me so that I can be poured out in blessings to others for His Glory.

This reminds me of 1 Cor. 12:3, which says, *"Therefore I tell you that no one who is speaking by the Spirit of God says, 'Jesus be cursed' and no one can say, 'Jesus is Lord' except by the Holy Spirit."*

What's in a Hug?
Or a Smile?

One Saturday evening I was doing my usual walk-about in church. I like to greet and talk to folks as they come in, and then I go around looking to see if anyone looks alone or at a loss, or just sitting by themselves.

I usually go up and introduce myself and ask how they are doing, or if they need prayer. This is just a way to make conversation and get to know people, and make them feel welcome in church. We have such a large congregation at Fort Lauderdale, and it is hard to find out if people are new or if they have been coming a while.

I was walking about when a friend of mine saw me and called me over to introduce me to a girl, whom she had just met and wanted me to meet her.

"Welcome to Calvary, you know God loves you, right?" I said as I gave her a big hug. Little did I know that this girl was contemplating suicide. It was only afterwards when I saw my friend again that she told me the girl was so surprised that I had said "God loves you" and gave her a hug. "She felt as if God had hugged her," my friend told me. "She felt His love through you."

I was shocked because I do this all the time and never know what people are going through. But I do know this. Years ago, God spoke to my heart about this. *"Your hugs will bring healing to some and make them feel secure in Me,"* He said. He also told me that my smile would bless many. *"Smile, love and hug on those whom I send your way,"* He said, and I have been doing this for years. But that was the first time that I know that my simple words and hugs saved a girl's life! So, my friends, if you are a hugger, or if you have a lovely smile, let the Lord use it for His glory. You never know when He will call on you to help save one of His dear children.

Another day, during one of our church's special events being held in the Sanctuary, a woman and her husband came up to me and said, "You have the most welcoming smile we have ever seen in a church. You have made us feel so welcome!"

"Praise the Lord," I said, not knowing what else to say.

"Well, it's working, thank you. Keep on smiling!" They said and off they went. You never know who's watching you, and when you let the Lord use you, a blessing always follows. Colossians 3:23 says, *"Do everything as unto God and not to man."* He will bless you if you do this.

Enriched by Him

The Healing Prayer of a Child

My daughter Sharon was only seven years old when this wonderful miracle took place. Let me retrace my steps a bit. The night before, I was with my friend Chris Greenman, the wonderful lady who had taking us all in to live with her when we first arrived in Florida.

Chris lived in Boca Raton in a beautiful big house that her late husband had built. It was late at night. Jim and the kids were already asleep, but Chris and I were up talking about not having seen instant healing on anyone that we had prayed for. We knew that it could happen, as we had read many of the Bible stories that talked about such miracles, especially in Jesus' time here on earth.

A few days after moving into our rented house, I invited Chris to be our first guest at our new house. I prepared a meal that we all loved—Shepherd's Pie.

"Let me show you all that God has provided for us," I said to Chris, as I opened all my cabinets to show her my dishes, and the rest of all the stuff I had received.

More on that in the next chapter!

"Look at this!" I pointed to my new toaster oven, then laid my hand on top of it with delight. Except, my enthusiasm got the best of me, as I had forgotten to turn off the oven.

My hand sizzled. Oh, the pain!

Chris immediately put my hand under the tap. Hot water came out. Oh, the pain!

Tears ran down my cheeks as I watched the blisters come up like grapes on my hand. We got ice from the icebox and it cooled it for a second before it melted. Jim and the boys heard the commotion and came into the kitchen. Sharon, who had been getting ready for bed, came running down from her room.

"I want to pray for mummy too!" So she put her hand on mine and asked a very specific prayer of the Lord: "Dear Jesus, please take the pain away from mummy's hand and take the swelling and blisters away and make it all better. Thank you, Jesus!"

Instantly, my hand was healed.

We all stood in shock.

Chris and I looked at each other and we could hardly believe it. Our precious Lord had come right into my kitchen and shown us He was very real and on time. Never late, never early, just right on time. I learned that day that when we pray in faith

Enriched by Him

believing just as child, He works.

I was so relieved; the pain was gone. We told the whole story to our pastor the following Saturday morning at our little prayer meeting. I showed him my hand and he couldn't believe it.

"Because Chris witnessed it, as well as Jim and the boys, I know that it happened," he said. A woman who was at the meeting stood up and showed us a burn mark on her arm where she had burned it taking something out of the oven.

"I did it two days ago and the mark and blisters are still there," she said, pointing to them.

Everyone was amazed at what God had done. Chris and I thanked him for showing us that He had heard our prayers. We knew that He wanted us to know that He is the same yesterday, today and forever (Hebrews 13:8).

He still heals people instantly when He sees fit to do so! So friends, come before Him in child like faith, as my daughter did, and see what happens. You may see a miracle too.

Furniture Delivery

Rain or Shine

Chris' daughter Debbie found us that nice big house for rent in Coral Springs. At first, the owner of that house did not want to rent to us because we had three kids. Somehow, Debbie not only convinced him that we would be good renters and taking care of the place, but she also got him to lower the rent by one hundred dollars. We lived in that house for seven years and the owner never raised the rent once. After we moved, we needed to furnish the place. So, our pastor made an announcement from the pulpit.

"The Goldie's need furniture!" To our astonishment, after the service was over several people came up to us and offered us all kinds of stuff, including a TV set, dishes, pots and pans, beds, table lamps, and various other things that enabled us to move in. We left church that day overwhelmed. We had all the essentials to begin our new life as a family once more. Dr. Lunsford, another good friend, had a beautiful couch, coffee table, and lamps for the living room plus a few other nice things that he wanted to give us, but the couch was extra long and heavy.

"How are we going to get it to our house?" we asked.

"I'll hitch up my boat to my car and we can load the things in the boat," he said. I had never heard of anyone moving furniture by boat, but this was America, after all.

What size of boat did he have? I wondered.

"There's only one problem," Dr. Lunsford said, and I thought that was an understatement, but said instead: "What's that?"

"Well, it looks like it's going to rain, and when it rains in South Florida, it rains! It comes on as quick as a wink and then goes off," he said, and he was right. I looked outside and the sky was very black, and seemed to get blacker by the minute.

"It sure doesn't look good," Dr. Lunsford said.

"The rain will stay off until we get to Coral Springs," I declared with the assurance that only God can give you. Dr. Lunsford gave me a look then said, "It's awfully dark up there. I'm not sure, Dot."

"You don't have to be sure. I have faith that it won't rain," I said.

"It's a long trip from Boca to Coral Springs," he warned.

"If it rains, all the stuff will be soaked through," he said, but I convinced him that we would get there dry, and so we loaded it into the boat. It must have looked so funny to anyone who saw us loading everything, like Noah building his boat. As you may recall from reading his story, people laughed at him.

I feel a bit like Noah right now, I thought, as I saw people passing by and smiling at us. Yes, they probably thought we were insane, but I didn't care.

Soon we were off, and I prayed the whole way. Flashes of lightning crossed the sky. Thunder roared, but no rain. We finally reached the house, and still no rain.

"That was unbelievable," Dr. Lunsford said. "All that thunder and lightning and no rain." He began to untie the ropes, with Jim and the boys' help, while Sharon and I made a cup of tea for everyone.

First things, first. Tea makes everything good. And that kind of prayer makes you thirsty! Just when Dr. Lunsford and the guys got everything unloaded and into the house, the heavens opened up and rain like I had never seen before poured down.

Dr. Lunsford was amazed. He stood in my doorway with his mouth wide open, as he watched the rain and flashes of lightning light up the Coral Springs sky.

"UN-BE-LIEV-ABLE," he said, over and over again.

I called out to him from the kitchen, "BE-LIEVE-IT! God is on His throne watching over His own!"

Enriched by Him

We closed the door and we all gave thanks to the Lord for holding off the rain until we had everything inside. Dr. Lunsford drove back to Boca a believer!

The Butcher in Budapest

One night in Budapest, I went out to dinner with friends and ended up sharing the Gospel with a butcher.

Jeremy and Christi Foster, who were missionaries at the castle in Vajta, had invited us to go to dinner at an Italian restaurant that they liked. So we agreed to go and have a nice couples night out on the town. Christi has Italian in her blood and loved the food there.

We were relaxed and just hanging out talking about food and the likes, when we got on the subject of steaks. I, being a butcher by trade, began giving my expert advice on what to buy and what not to buy. We chatted about that at length until it was time to go. We went on a walk around the mall, where Jim offered to buy us all a coffee.

Christie and I got a table, and while we were waiting for the guys I looked around and saw a couple of shops close by. One of them was a butcher's shop. I strolled over to look at the display in the window. The butcher behind the counter was watching and made a gesture to see if I wanted to buy anything. I called Jeremy over to look at the steaks he had on display, and as I was explaining to him what was the best kind to buy, the butcher came up to us.

"Can I help you with anything?" He asked, but I explained that I was a butcher and was showing Jeremy the best cuts to buy for frying or grilling. The butcher was taken aback that I was a butcher and called his manager out front to talk to me.

He offered me a job.

"I'm on vacation and will be going home in a few days," I explained.

"I can give you a job for a month if you want it," he insisted.

"You speak English well," I said, changing the subject.

"I learned it at a Catholic school," he said and that opened up the conversation about the Lord.

"Do you know Jesus as your personal Savior?" I asked.

"Are you Jewish?" He asked because he saw my necklace. That began the conversation about Jesus.

"I went through all the Catholic stuff but I don't like the way they worshipped idols," he said.

"Would you like to get to know Jesus in a more personal way?" I asked and soon saw myself sharing the Gospel with him. The Lord used us to clarify all the things that the butcher had misunderstood. He had left the Catholic Church and was now going to the Reform Church in Budapest, but he found things not quite right there either. So again, we shared more back and forth, answering all his questions that he had.

"I'm a pastor," Jeremy told him. "Some of the teaching you've had is a bit mixed up, so just read your Bible if you have one."

"I do have one," the butcher said, and promised that he would go home that night and ask Jesus to reveal himself to him through John's Gospel. He showed us a cross that he carried in his wallet.

"I want to show you something," the butcher said, and Jeremy's eyebrows shot up.

"I hope you are not going to show us a picture of Jesus," Jeremy said.

"No, no!" the butcher said as pulled out a cross necklace.

"That's nice," I said to him. "But the cross is empty?"

"Well, Jesus is dead," he said.

"No!" I said. "Jesus is alive and lives in Heaven. He will return soon to take us home with Him. But first we must know Him as our Savior." We shared the prayer of salvation with him that night but he still had many questions.

"Come to our church," Jeremy said, inviting him to come to Calvary Chapel in Budapest.

Enriched by Him

"I know where it is. I will come one night and try it," the butcher said.

We believe he was really seeking the Lord and we prayed with him before parting company. I can't go into all the details that took place that night except to say, that guy heard the Gospel for the first time in his life. And I truly believe he did read his Bible that night. He was so sincere in asking his questions. He wanted to know the truth, as most people do. We told him the truth was Jesus.

Two Long Weekends at the Florida Keys

"Jim, will you build me some cabinets for my house at the Keys?" Dr. Joe Lunsford asked Jim one day.

"I would be happy to do this," Jim replied.

Jim Built the furniture out in our garage at home, and when he was finished Joe asked him to install them at his house in the Keys.

"Yes, of course," Jim said, so both families went together for the weekend. We didn't stay at the house. Joe had booked us into a hotel. The next day we all went fishing. Joe and his girls had all the poles and bait, and they showed us how to use them, as I'd never fished before, and neither had Jim or Sharon.

Fishing was actually a lot of fun. We each caught something and then threw it back in. Meanwhile, Jim had done all the carpentry work, so later that night we went out to dinner. Joe treated us to a real fish dinner at a real cool restaurant, and afterwards we went back to the hotel. It was a real nice, exotic Hawaiian type of place right on the water, and at night you could hear the waves lapping up on the shore. One thing you can't miss about the Keys is the heat. It is tremendous! It comes out of the ground and engulfs you from your feet all the way up to your scalp. If you are not careful you can melt right there on the pavement. It drains you. It tires you. And you want nothing but a nice refreshing pool to soothe your sun-kissed skin. Jim and I felt like millionaires staying at a place like that!

The next morning we went back to the house. Jim worked on installing the cabinets while Kenny and I, along with the kids, enjoyed the Gulf of Mexico. When Jim was done with work, we sat on the balcony overlooking the Gulf eating a lunch that Kenny had prepared.

"Thank you, Lord Jesus for this wonderful time we are all having together," I praised. The house was so peaceful. It had been built up high on concrete blocks so that if the water rose, it would not get flooded.

Under the house there was a little guest apartment. It was all so lovely that I was just amazed that one family could have two homes like this, and still have money to spend. And here we were being blessed by this wonderful family and getting all this treatment for free. God is so good.

The girls had a blast running in and out of the water for hours. Then when Jim got finished again, Joe took us on a trip to see "The African Queen," a boat that was used in the film by the same name with Humphrey Bogart. Perhaps not too many of you will remember him. He played in a lot of gangster movies when I was growing up. We took some pictures for a memory of it all. Then Joe took us to a place similar to Sea World, where the girls could pet seals and sea lions. We had a super time there and made lots of good memories. Joe took us sightseeing all around town, and it was wonderful!

Joe pulled Jim aside when he finished working that weekend. "I would like to give you guys a treat," Joe told Jim.

What treat? This whole weekend had been a treat as far as we were concerned!

"Now that everything is finished, I want you to have a weekend by yourselves here at the house," Joe said.

He gave Jim the key to the house and we went down there for St. Patrick's Day weekend. No kids. Just Jim and me! Oh, it was glorious. The weather was perfect. We felt like royalty, living in this beautiful house.

God is so good.

We enjoyed the beach and the peace of that place. I cooked the meals, as we couldn't afford the fancy restaurants down there. But it was great, because I love to cook. Jim always says, "I love Dot's Kitchen better than anywhere else!"

Enriched by Him

What a guy! I love him.

We sat on the patio and just watched the sun go down at night. The sky was so beautiful. The hues of gold and purple and yellow were magnificent.

God is an awesome artist.

The lapping of the waves broke the quiet, like a sweet lullaby. It was so good. God truly blessed us by giving us kind and generous friends like Joe and Kenny. Jim and I took photos of that week and they hang in our living room to this day.

As I was writing this chapter, Sharon, who is now 39, looked through some old photos to show her little girls. She came across the African Queen pictures when she was just seven years old. All the memories of that day flooded back as if it had been yesterday.

Bath Bowls and Basins

One morning I woke up and heard the Lord say to me, *"Bath Bowls and Basins!"* I got up out of bed and went to the bathroom and as I looked in the mirror it was as if the Lord said to me, *"Look into your eyes."* So, I did. Then He said again, *"Baths Bowls and Basins."*

I asked, "What about them Lord?"

"I am going to show you that you can have a perfect day with Me. Only do what I tell you to do and when you go to bed tonight you will see how bright your eyes are and you will not be wiped out! Your body will not be weary from over exertion."

So my day began. First, I had my quiet time with the Lord, then I got showered and dressed. As I heard earlier, I was to clean the bathrooms first, bath bowls and basin, then just as I was about to clean the mirror, as I always did, that small voice in my head said, *"Ah! Bath bowls and basins! Leave the mirror until tonight. When you are getting ready to go to bed you will look in it and see what I have done,"* the Lord said. So I left the mirror!

Enriched by Him

Just as I was about to ask, "What's next, Lord?"

"Go downstairs and make tea," He said. "You have a friend coming to see you."

I do? I didn't know that.

I didn't argue with the Lord, I just went down and put the kettle on for tea, as that is how we do it in Scotland. Just then the phone rang. It was my friend Pat Barron. She is an English lady, but I don't hold that against her! [That was a wee joke.]

"I want to come over to talk to you," said Pat, but not much more than that.

"Come on over and have a wee cup of tea. It will be ready by the time you get here," I told her. When I hung up the phone I began to pick up papers to put it in the rack, and the Lord said, *"Don't do anything else, just put the papers away—then spray the living room with air freshner. That's all!"*

I said, "Lord…" Then, I heard the kettle's whistle, so I made the tea and just when I was about to turn, the doorbell rang. It was Pat. The fist thing she said as she stepped in the front door was, "Your house is so nice and clean."

I had only done baths bowls and basins, and tidied up the papers, and sprayed the fresh air stuff. I didn't say anything to her about B, B, and B.

"God told me to come to your house and that you were to

pray for me," she explained the reason for her visit. She had had an accident! She got her hand jammed in a car door. She thought her three fingers were broken.

"God told me that if you prayed for me, He would heal me," she said.

After I prayed for her, I told her, "You have more faith than me Pat, but I'll pray for you anyway." We sat down at the table in my dining room. The sun was shining in through the glass sliding windows. The house was filled with light. I began to pray.

"Lord, please heal Pat's fingers," I prayed as I anointed her with cooking oil then prayed for her healing.

As soon as I finished, Pat instantly unraveled the splint and bandages she had on her fingers and put them on the table. She began to bend and flex her fingers as though nothing was wrong with them. They were healed! God did a miracle right there in front of our eyes.

God is so good!

We sat there and had our tea and praised Him for his goodness and healing. Then, I told Pat about what the Lord had told me that morning. She was ecstatic! She knew God was going to heal her and she could not stop talking. Eventually, we quieted down and had a time of prayer together. Time flew by and it was now 3 P.M. Sharon came home from school, and she had brought a friend with her. "Mommy, will you pray for her to accept Jesus as her Savior?"

"Honey, you can do it," I encouraged her. "You don't need me!"

"Please, mommy…" Sharon insisted, as her friend Tori had been asking her about Jesus. Sharon had told Tori that I could tell her what she needed to know. So I shared the Gospel with the little girl, and she gave her heart to Jesus.

"Thank you for praying for me," Tori said smiling.

"Be sure you tell your parents what you did," I told her. "And your friends so that they too might come to know Jesus." Tori promised she would and left with a big smile on her face. Sharon was so happy now that her friend was a Christian.

"You know, Sharon, you could lead people to the Lord," I told her. "You don't need anyone else!" I assured her.

"I don't know if I can do it," she said.

"Whatever you say will be alright," I said. "If your heart is right with Jesus, He will give you the words to speak." From that day, she led all her friends to the Lord by herself. She has never asked me again. Praise the Lord!

After all that, Sharon got ready to go to gymnastics. As I was in the kitchen with Pat, preparing a Shepherds Pie for dinner, when my son Alan came home from school. I asked if he would take Sharon to the gym, and he was happy to do it. We told Alan all that the Lord had done before he came home and he was amazed. Soon Jim and Derek got home from work, and we shared our day with them. "I had a near miss at work," Jim said. "I was cutting a piece of wood on the saw and it went flying in the air, nearly missing my eye!"

"What time was it when that happened?" I asked. From what he said, it had been when Pat and I were praying. Derek also had an incident at Publix, where he worked. "I was helping unload a pallet when all of a sudden it began to fall over," he said. "I managed to side step it, and it missed me by inches when it fell."

"What time did this happen?" I asked again, and again it was the same answer: when we were praying for him at work.

What a day! Near misses, healing, and a nice bright house without cleaning, and on top of that, a little girl getting saved. Praise the Lord! *What's next?* I wondered.

Alan came home after taking Sharon to the gym, and told us of an "incident" that happened on Wiles Road. "A truck was in front of me carrying Christmas trees, with a man sitting in the back holding the trees in place. One of the trees fell out of the back of the truck right into my path," he said. "I had to swerve onto the grassy verge at the side of the road and just missed hitting another car!"

Enriched by Him

The truck never stopped. Alan was safe, praise God again!

Later that night, when I went to pick up Sharon from the gym, I learned that she had fallen from the bars practicing a new move. She hurt her back and was winded, but after praying for her, she was fine.

Pat went home. And as I closed the door I sent a silent prayer up to Heaven. My family was safely home. No one was happier than me. I thought of all that happened that day and more importantly, what could have happened. God was with us. Greater is He who is in us than he who is in the world.

The house was quiet. Everyone had gone to sleep. I was getting ready to go to bed when I heard that small quiet voice say to me, *"Go into the bathroom and look in the mirror,"* He said. *"You can clean the mirror now."*

So I cleaned it. Then the Lord said, *"Look at your eyes."* So I did. They were bright and shining, not tired at all. I felt so great it was unbelievable. No aches or pains anywhere. I praised God for a wee while for all His goodness to us that day. Everything was done just as He had said, and I did have a perfect day. I did only what He told me to do and nothing more. It was awesome. It's good to be obedient, knowing that God delights in that. He sends His angels to watch over us all the time. Praise God!

Pat's Second Healing

"Can you and Maria come over and pray for my mom?" Pat's daughter Chantelle asked me one day. "My mom can't move. She can't even get out of her bed," she said. Pat had asked her daughter to call me because she knew that Maria and I prayed every Monday from 9 A.M. to 3 P.M., no matter what.

"I'll call Maria and we will be there soon if that's what God wants us to do," I said. "I'll call you back after Maria and I pray."

After Maria and I prayed, we called Chantelle back. "We're on our way!" I said.

As I prayed on the way to get Maria, I looked up at the clouds in front of me. It looked like a man raising someone up out of a bed. I told Maria when I got to her place and she confirmed the vision to me.

"The Lord told me we should go!" Maria said. She was reading about how the Lord raised up a little girl in her daily reading that morning. We both were excited as to what God was going to do.

Enriched by Him

We set out for Pat's house over in Lighthouse Point, and we prayed all the way there. "Lord, what do you wants us to do?" we prayed. "Please, glorify Yourself in all this."

When we reached the house Chantelle let us in. There was another couple there from Spanish River, Pat's church. They were sitting by her bed and another woman was standing at the bottom of the bed. They too had come to pray for Pat.

As soon as they saw us they said, "The second shift has arrived!"

Pat looked awful. She was grey looking and in a lot of pain.

"Please lay hands on me!" She cried out to us as we came in.

"We have already done that and they tried to lift her up, but she screamed," the couple said. Pat couldn't stand the pain, so they put her back down on the bed.

Pat looked up at us, repeating, "Lay hands on me!"

"Pat, we are going to do whatever the Lord wants us to do, not what you want," I said. "We can't do anything on our own," I explained. "Do you want God to do something or us?"

I was very bold. I could hardly believe I was saying these things to her.

"We have to go," said the couple and then left. The other woman stayed. Maria and I began to pray asking the Lord for His guidance. The other woman that was there began to pray out loud in tongues. I felt like the Lord said to me, *"Tell her to be quiet."*

I said to her, "Be quiet!"

She looked at me and said, "I am praying for Pat!"

"Do it in the other room," I said in a commanding voice. And off she went. Maria and I were amazed when we felt the Lord saying, *"Now you can work!"*

Maria stood at the bottom of the bed and I stood at the headboard. We prayed over Pat and anointed her with oil, then waited on the Lord. Maria prayed in Spanish, which is her native tongue. It was easier for her to pray in Spanish, and I prayed in Scottish, my native tongue!

"Lord, please tell us what to do," we prayed. "Show us how you want things done." Step by step we went through the process and then the Lord clearly said, *"Tell her to get up!"* So I said to Pat, "The Lord says, *'Get up!'*" And she did.

No pain anywhere. Pat got up and danced all around the room, praising God. The woman in the next room came in and saw Pat dancing.

"What happened?" She said. "We prayed all morning for her and nothing, and now she's dancing! You are healed!" She said as she looked at Pat, and then at us. "How did you do this?"

Both Maria and I said almost in unison, "We didn't do

Enriched by Him

anything. God did. That's what happened!" The woman was amazed. She had never seen anything like this before. She started speaking in tongues again over and over, and then she left to tell the others what had happened.

God had healed Pat.

"Get dressed," I told Pat.

"I'll just rest in bed," she said.

"Why? You're not sick. Get dressed!" I said with a boldness I didn't know I had. "We will wait in the kitchen."

Pat called Chantelle to tell her what happened. She came home for lunch and saw her mom up and dancing!

"Mom is okay now," Chantelle called her sister on the phone to give her the good news. Everyone was happy. We had lunch and praised God for His miracle working power. We stayed with Pat for a while after lunch, then she started feeling some discomfort on her back again. We prayed immediately and the Lord said, *"Tell her to lie down on the floor and roll back and forward from side to side."*

We went into the living room and Pat laid on the floor and rolled from side to side. I had to laugh a wee bit because I felt like it was like telling your dog to roll over! The Lord said, *"Tell her to get up,"* and so I told her, "Get Up!" She held her hand out for me to help her up but the Lord said, *"She has to lean on*

Me, not on you." Pat rolled onto her side and lifted herself up, and as she got to her feet the pain was gone! She never had another bit of trouble with her back again. The Lord healed her completely.

Jeremiah 17:14 says, *"Heal me Lord and I will be healed. Save me and I will be saved for you are the one I praise."* And Jeremiah 30:17 says, *"I will restore you to health and heal your wounds, declares the Lord."*

Prayer is our direct line to God, the Creator of the universe, but also our Abba Father—our Daddy. The Lord has told me to teach people how to pray. This is my message. This is my mission. It's not what I say, but the words He gives me. Likewise, when you pray, it's not your words, but His that have the power to change and enrich your life and that of others.

My Mom's Last Words To Me

I was already in Florida when I got word from my family in Scotland that my mom was in the hospital. I couldn't get to see her because I didn't have the money to fly back home. So, I called her up on the telephone and the hospital switchboard put me through to her ward.

In Scotland, only nurse stations have telephones. So the nurse brought my mom to the phone. By the time she reached the nurse station, she was out of breath but managed to talk to me for a few minutes.

"Mom, I am praying for you every day," I told her.

She said, "I'm fine. You just keep doing what He tells you to do."

"I love you mom," I said. We hung up the phone with that because she couldn't do anymore. I never heard my mom's voice after that. A few days later, a friend of ours heard of my dilemma of not being able to go visit my mom in her last few days and bought me a ticket to go to Scotland. I was so grateful for that.

Dot Goldie

I set off for Scotland, and when I arrived I went right to the hospital with my brother Harris. Mom was sleeping when we went in. My brother gently woke her from her sleep and quietly said, "Look who's here to see you. It's Dot! She's come from America."

My mom looked, her eyes wide open. She smiled. Harris asked her, "Do you recognize her?"

She nodded yes and smiled. I visited her daily, but she was unconscious on the last day I saw her. I leaned over her and whispered in her ear, "Go home mom, Jesus is waiting for you. I'll see you in a wee while. Don't hang on here anymore. Go to Jesus."

I left the hospital, tears running down my cheeks but they were tears of joy for my mom was going to be with Jesus and I would see her again someday.

That night I was praying with my brother and sister-in-law and we released my mom into the Lord's hands. At 1:00 A.M. in the morning my mom passed away. I was in bed, reading the Bible when the phone call came. The first thing that came to mind was a time when my mom had danced with one of the pastors in the Church of England at a celebration. I could just picture her, smiling as she danced. *She will be dancing with Jesus now*, I thought.

Enriched by Him

An hour before that, Harris had prayed a very short prayer, simply saying, "Into Your hands Lord, I commit my mother." Harris later said that that was the quickest answer he ever got.

I had the privilege of leading both my mom and dad to the Lord so I will see them both again one day soon. Do you have that hope? I hope so! Now praise Him!

Becoming a Christian begins with the surrender of our hearts to Jesus and believing that He died for our sins, ascended into Heaven and is seated at His Father's right hand, but that's not all.

It's so important to realize at the begining of our Christian walk that we need to keep walking, even when we think there's no place to get to. Nothing other than the revealed truth of Christ is solid and strong enough to form a foundation that will enrich our lives and direct our every step. Without it there's only fear and a world of counfusion. Of people wondering why they are here or if they've totally missed their purpose in life.

Can you imagine the hoplessnes of trying to live a Christian life when you're constantly looking up at the skies, not looking for direction but to surf the clouds, miserably, looking for signs of great weather? Because you know that's what the world does.

I have found that life is about giving in to all those things we can't control, and surrender to the One—"who is, and who was, and who is to come" Revelation 1:4. Everything that you want He can provide, if it is according to His will. Anything that you can dream, He can make come true. So, seek it. Ask it. Believe it. He will do it. Then, be thanful.

What are you most grateful for? Your mother and father? Your spouse and kids? Your career? Your Finances? Your friends? God created all of it. Tell Him that you know that He is the source of all the goodness and treasures in your life. Give Him the glory!

As I think of my mom and the last words she said to me; everyting that I am, everything that I do or will do, comes into perspective. "You just keep doing what He tells you to do," she said. And she was right.

There's something so tender about this to me, about resting in His care, just like I rested in her loving arms when I was a child. Listening to Him the way I listened to her, because I trusted that she knew what was best for me. And in my walk with Jesus there's that hope, that belief that He knows me, that He loves me, and will continue to protect and provide for me and my family all the days of my life. What more can a wee woman want?

About the Author

Dot was born in Glasgow, Scotland. She has been a missionary for many years in Scotland, England, Eastern Europe, South and Central America, India, as well as Africa, sharing the Gospel wherever she goes. God spoke to her about writing a book, and she tried to put it off for many years, until finally she sat down one summer day and wrote her first book, *The Encourager,* to be followed by this one. She hopes that her words will bless and encourage her readers, and that God will use them in the same way He has used her.

Dot lives in Florida and works at Calvary Chapel Fort Lauderdale's Outreach Ministry doing Missionary Care with her husband Jim. She is also a breast cancer survivor, and God has used this to encourage many other people she's met while going through this trial.

Whether writing about her family, old friends, miracles or her adventures with Jesus, in or off the mission field, she shows us the myriad ways her faith guides and sustains her. God is real to Dot and she wants the world to know Him like that.

www.ingramcontent.com/pod-product-compliance
Lightning Source LLC
Chambersburg PA
CBHW061656040426
42446CB00010B/1758